International Workshop on Resources and Techniques for User Information in Abusive Language Analysis (ResT-UP 2)

Held at LREC 2022

Marseille, France
20 – 25 June 2022

Editors:

Johanna Monti
Valerio Basile
Maria Pia Di Buono
Raffaele Manna
Antonio Pascucci
Sara Tonelli

ISBN: 978-1-7138-6135-5

Printed from e-media with permission by:

Curran Associates, Inc.
57 Morehouse Lane
Red Hook, NY 12571

CURRAN ASSOCIATES INC.
proceedings
.com

Some format issues inherent in the e-media version may also appear in this print version.

Association for Computational Linguistics
209 N. Eighth Street
Stroudsburg, Pennsylvania 18360

Phone: 1-570-476-8006
Fax: 1-570-476-0860

acl@aclweb.org

Additional copies of this publication are available from:

Curran Associates, Inc.
57 Morehouse Lane
Red Hook, NY 12571 USA
Phone: 845-758-0400
Fax: 845-758-2633
Email: curran@proceedings.com
Web: www.proceedings.com

LREC 2022 Workshop
Language Resources and Evaluation Conference
20-25 June 2022

International Workshop on Resources and Techniques for User Information in Abusive Language Analysis (ResT-UP 2)

PROCEEDINGS

Editors:
Johanna Monti, Valerio Basile, Maria Pia Di Buono, Raffaele Manna, Antonio Pascucci, Sara Tonelli

Proceedings of the LREC 2022 workshop on Resources and Techniques for User Information in Abusive Language Analysis (ResT-UP 2022)

Edited by: Johanna Monti, Valerio Basile, Maria Pia Di Buono, Raffaele Manna, Antonio Pascucci, Sara Tonelli

For more information:
European Language Resources Association (ELRA)
9 rue des Cordelières
75013, Paris
France
http://www.elra.info
Email: lrec@elda.org

Preface by the Workshop Organizers

Welcome to the LREC2022 Workshop on Resources and Techniques for User Information in Abusive Language Analysis (ResT-UP 2).

This volume documents the Proceedings of the Second International Workshop on Resources and Techniques for User Information in Abusive Language Analysis (ResT-UP 2), held on 24 June 2022 in Marseille (France) in conjunction with the LREC 2022 conference (International Conference on Language Resources and Evaluation).

The workshop aims at bringing together researchers and scholars working on author profiling and automatic detection of abusive language on the Web, e.g., cyberbullying or hate speech, with a twofold objective: improving existing LRs, e.g., datasets, corpora, lexicons, and sharing ideas on stylometry techniques and features useful to characterize abusive language online in a fair and transparent way. ResT-UP 2 targets Profiling scholars and research groups, experts in Statistical and Stylistic Analysis of texts as well as computational linguists who investigate author profiling and personality both in short texts (social media posts, blog texts and email) and in long texts (such as pamphlets, (fake) news and political documents). ResT-UP 2 represented an opportunity to share profiling experiments with the scientific community and to show automatic detection techniques of abusive language on the Web.

The workshop has been held as a hybrid event: the workshop was attended by about fifty people (onsite and remotely) between workshop organizers, panelists, keynote speakers and representatives of academic and industrial organizations.

The programme included four oral presentations and two keynote speakers: Viviana Patti and Walter Daelemans.
We would like to thank the invited speakers, all authors who contributed papers to this workshop edition, the Programme Committee members who provided valuable feedback during the review process and the LREC 2022 conference organizing committee.

Johanna Monti – L'Orientale University of Naples – UNIOR NLP Research Group
Valerio Basile – University of Turin – Content-centered Computing group
Maria Pia Di Buono – L'Orientale University of Naples – UNIOR NLP Research Group
Raffaele Manna – L'Orientale University of Naples – UNIOR NLP Research Group
Antonio Pascucci – L'Orientale University of Naples – UNIOR NLP Research Group
Sara Tonelli – Fondazione Bruno Kessler – Digital Humanities research group

- **Organizers:**

Johanna Monti – L'Orientale University of Naples – UNIOR NLP Research Group
Valerio Basile – University of Turin - Content-centered Computing group
Maria Pia Di Buono – L'Orientale University of Naples – UNIOR NLP Research Group
Raffaele Manna – L'Orientale University of Naples – UNIOR NLP Research Group
Antonio Pascucci – L'Orientale University of Naples – UNIOR NLP Research Group
Sara Tonelli – Fondazione Bruno Kessler, Digital Humanities research group

- **Program Committee:**

Cristina Bosco, University of Turin (ITALY)
Maciej Eder, Institute of Polish Language (Polish Academy of Sciences) (POLAND)
Francesca Frontini, Istituto di Linguistica Computazionale "A. Zampolli" - CNR & CLARIN ERIC (ITALY)
Stefano Menini, Fondazione Bruno Kessler (ITALY)
Suzanne Mpouli, Université de Paris (FRANCE)
Michael Oakes, University of Wolverhampton (UNITED KINGDOM)
Alessio Palmero Aprosio, Fondazione Bruno Kessler (ITALY)
Marco Polignano, University of Bari (ITALY)
Paolo Rosso, Universitat Politècnica de València (SPAIN)
Manuela Sanguinetti, University of Cagliari (ITALY)
Efstathios Stamatatos, University of Aegean (GREECE)
Arkaitz Zubiaga, Queen Mary University of London (UNITED KINGDOM)

- **Keynote Speakers:**

Walter Daelemans - Universiteit Antwerpen (BELGIUM)
Viviana Patti - University of Turin (ITALY)

Table of Contents

Conference Program

Proceedings of the ResT-UP2 Proceedings @LREC2022, pages 1–7
Marseille, 20-25 June 2022

A First Attempt at Unreliable News Detection in Swedish

Ricardo Muñoz Sánchez[1*], Eric Johansson[2*], Shakila Tayefeh[2*], Shreyash Kad[2*]
[1]The University of Gothenburg, [2]Chalmers University of Technology
Gothenburg, Sweden
ricardo.munoz.sanchez@svenska.gu.se, {ericjoha, tayefeh, shreyash}@student.chalmers.se

Abstract

Throughout the COVID-19 pandemic, a parallel infodemic has also been going on such that the information has been spreading faster than the virus itself. During this time, every individual needs to access accurate news in order to take corresponding protective measures, regardless of their country of origin or the language they speak, as misinformation can cause significant loss to not only individuals but also society. In this paper we train several machine learning models (ranging from traditional machine learning to deep learning) to try to determine whether news articles come from either a reliable or an unreliable source, using just the body of the article. Moreover, we use a previously introduced corpus of news in Swedish related to the COVID-19 pandemic for the classification task. Given that our dataset is both unbalanced and small, we use subsampling and easy data augmentation (EDA) to try to solve these issues. In the end, we realize that, due to the small size of our dataset, using traditional machine learning along with data augmentation yields results that rival those of transformer models such as BERT.

Keywords: Text categorisation, Less-resourced languages, Statistical and Machine Learning Methods

1. Introduction

Even though misinformation in media has existed for a long time, the digital era has allowed for it to have a wider reach, as was seen during Brexit and the U.S. presidential elections from 2016 and 2020. This has been exacerbated during the COVID-19 pandemic amid the uncertainty and length of this event. During his speech at the Munich Security Conference 2020, Tedros Adhanom Ghebreyesus (2020), general-director of the World Health Organization (WHO), used the term "infodemic" to characterize this viral spread of misinformation in a parallel manner to the actual pandemic . This has had real world effects, such as anti-lockdown demonstrations (Wikipedia, 2022) and the rise of more wide-spread anti-vax movements (Baer, 2021). As with most countries, Sweden has been no stranger to these (Glad and Sundberg, 2021).

In this paper we work with news articles related to the COVID-19 pandemic in Swedish coming from reliable and unreliable sources. We use traditional and neural models to attempt to determine whether a given article comes from an reliable or an unreliable source. Given that our dataset is unbalanced, we also explore three different kinds of data augmentation (subsampling, backtranslation, and easy data augmentation) to attempt to solve the issues caused by this. The dataset we use was originally presented by Kokkinakis (2021) but to the best of our knowledge, it hasn't been used since its introduction. More information about the dataset itself can be found in section 3. On the other hand, we describe our data augmentation methods in section 3.1 and the models that we use for classification in section 4.

We observe that a logistic regression model with tf-idf representations performs the best at detecting previously unseen unreliable articles, while maintaining a good overall F1-score. This model outperforms BERT and other models such as LSTMs and SVMs. We also realize that easy data augmentation (EDA) tends to improve the results of the models in most cases. Due to these surprising results, we conclude that the current dataset is too small and the more complex models are probably overfitting the training data.

2. Background

Several tasks have arisen in the NLP community to try to study mis- and disinformation. In this section we will give a brief overview of them, as well as some of the methods that have been used to tackle these tasks. Even though we are studying news coming from unreliable sources, two closely related tasks exist.

In fake news detection, we try to determine whether a news article is intentionally deceptive. However, this requires us to know the intent of the person writing it, so is is often reduced to whether an article is truthful or not (Oshikawa et al., 2020). One way to do this is through simple classification of the titles and text of the articles has been attempted, both with traditional machine learning ((Shu et al., 2020) uses these as baselines) and with deep learning (see for example (Raza, 2021)) approaches. However, fact verification has also been successfully used for this task (Vijjali et al., 2020). Torabi Asr and Taboada (2018) note that it is important for fake news to have annotations the epistemological truth value of each article rather than on a source level. Because of that, we consider our task to be detection of news coming from unreliable sources rather than fake news detection, despite using similar methods and approaches.

*All authors had equal contribution. Correspondence to ricardo.munoz.sanchez@svenska.gu.se

Dataset description			
Split	Total size	Reliable	Unreliable
Train	1399	1259	140
Validation	298	269	29
Test	296	268	28

Table 1: Number of articles in each of the splits.

On the other hand, rumour mining focuses on unproven claims, often on social media. While the task can be seen as text classification (as task 8 of SemEval-2017 (Derczynski et al., 2017)), there have been people that have studied how rumours spread (see (Ma et al., 2018) for an example).
Other related tasks include detection of hyper-partisan news, stance, clickbait, satire, and propaganda.

3. Dataset

We use a dataset that was originally introduced in (Kokkinakis, 2021). This is a dataset that contains "news" related to the pandemic coming from different sources. These vary from official announcements from the government, to blogs that usually post articles about conspiracy theories. While the text of the articles is not freely available for download due to copyright, individual sentences can be accessed in a randomized order through Korp, the corpus search interface from SpråkbankenText[1] (Borin et al., 2012).
While the original dataset has more fine-grained labels, we grouped them into reliable sources and unreliable sources. A thorough list of the reliable and of the unreliable sources can be found in Tables 2 and 3, respectively, as well as a short description of most of them.
The dataset itself consists of the titles and the texts of each article, as well as other metadata such as the date it was published on and the URL of the article. Given that our dataset does not contain a thorough compilation of all COVID-19 articles that have been published in Swedish (neither by source nor by date), we just used the text and the titles for our classification task.
There are 1796 articles coming from reliable sources and 198 coming from unreliable ones in the dataset. In order to create a train/validation/test split, we randomly selected articles such that there was a similar proportion of official to unofficial articles in each split. The actual size of the splits can be seen in Table 1. We decided against the recommendation of Zhou et al. (2021) of not letting the same source appear in more than one split, as it would have meant that the validation and test sets would have consisted mainly of a single source due to the small size of our dataset, which could have also skewed our results.

3.1. Data Augmentation

As mentioned previously, our dataset has two important limitations: it is unbalanced and has a small number of examples of unreliable articles. In order to get around these limitations, we tried three different ways of data augmentation: subsampling of the reliable class and using a combination of backtranslation and EDA.

3.1.1. Subsampling

Given that there are about ten reliable sources for each unreliable one, one of the risks when training is that the model will decide that every article is reliable and still achieve a high accuracy. This poses a problem in alignment (Ortega et al., 2018), that is, when an AI model follows the rules that we set for it but doesn't do what we expect it to do. In other words, it learns how to "cheat" in order to get better results.

3.1.2. Backtranslation

Backtranslation (Edunov et al., 2018) is a simple augmentation method where synthetic data is generated by translating the original text into another language and then back into the original language. The intention is that the generated text retains the context of the original sentence but with different words and phrases. For this we use an API to access Google Translate[2].

3.1.3. Easy Data Augmentation (EDA)

Easy data augmentation (EDA) consists of four simple operations described in the original paper (Wei and Zou, 2019) as follows

- **Synonym replacement** Randomly select n words from the sentence that are not stop words. Replace each of these words with one of its synonyms chosen at random.
- **random insertion:** Find a random synonym of a random word in the sentence that is not a stop word. Insert that synonym into a random position in the sentence. Repeat this process n times.
- **random swap:** Randomly choose two words in the sentence and swap their positions. Repeat this process n times.
- **random deletion:** For each word in the sentences, randomly remove it from the sentence with probability p.

Parameters n and p determine the amount of noise to be added to the newly generated sentences. The original paper argues that, if we have a small dataset, using EDA on 50% of the training data can outperform the results from using the whole training data. We used the code from the authors' GitHub repository[3].

3.2. Training Sets

Using the augmentation techniques in the previous section, we obtain a total of four different training sets constructed from the original one. These new sets are as follows:

[1] https://spraakbanken.gu.se/korp/#?corpus=sv-covid-19

[2] https://github.com/lushan88a/google_trans_new

[3] https://github.com/jasonwei20/eda_nlp

Source	Description
Sveriges Radio	Swedish public service radio
Socialstyrelsen	The National Board of Health and Welfare
Myndigheten för Samhällskydd och Beredskap (msb)	The Agency for Civil Protection and Emergency Planning
Folkhälsomyndigheten	Swedish public health authority
Riksdagen	Swedish parliament
Regeringen	Swedish government
Krisinformation	Crisis information
Dagens Industri (di)	Liberal-conservative financial newspaper
Ehälsomyndigheten	Swedish e-Health agency
Göteborgsposten (gp)	Liberal, daily newspaper
Dagens Nyheter (dn)	Independently liberal newspaper
Vi	Monthly magazine on culture and society
Svenska Dagbladet (svd)	Independent moderate, daily newspaper
Hälsingborgs Dagblad (hd)	Largest Swedish daily newspaper outside of the metropolitan districts of Stockholm, Gothenburg, and Malmö
Västerbottenkuriren (vk.se, blogg.vk.se)	Swedish daily newspaper published in Västerbotten

Table 2: A list of the reliable sources, as well as a short description for most of them.

Source	Description
Anthropocene	'A politically independent, liberal forum for debate and opinion formation'
Det Goda Samhället	Online publication for which the financing takes place with the help of grants from private individuals and companies
Fria Tider	Immigration-critical online newspaper
Nyadagbladet	A Swedish online newspaper founded in 2012 which is nationalist, science-skeptical, and non-partisan.
Swebbtv	Swedish media channel, the channel describes itself as being politically independent and critical of Sweden's immigration policy
kavlaner.se	Anti vaccination campaign
humanismkunskap.org	(No description available)
sv.technocracy.news	Proponents of technocracy, tend to be very conspiratorial regarding COVID-19
frihetsportalen.se	'This site is produced by Mats Jangdal in Sweden and mainly in Swedish. Occasionally I publish in English. The site is devoted to topics like freedom, property rights and the UN climate fraud, also politics in general.'
static.bloggproffs.se	(No description available)
cornucopia.cornubot.se	'... The blog's ambition is to be wrong in everything [sic]. By writing about potential problems before they arise or worsen, we may be able to avoid them or reduce their consequences ...'
newsvoice.se	' ... NewsVoice does not shy away from exposing corruption and abuse of power and is therefore not politically correct ...'
trovetandeochvetenskap.se	Blog with the subheading: 'Only those who swim against the current reach the source'

Table 3: A list of the unreliable sources, as well as a short description for most of them.

1. The unchanged original training set.

2. For each unreliable data point in training set 1, one new data point is generated by backtranslation and five new data points through a combination of backtranslation and EDA.

3. A balanced training set extracted from the original one by subsampling the reliable articles.

4. Data augmentation as in training set 2 is performed to all data points from training set 3.

The original validation and test sets are used in their

original forms throughout the training and evaluation of all models.

4. Models for Text Classification

We compare several kinds of models to determine which one has the best performance.

4.1. Logistic Regression

In order to establish a baseline, we used a logistic regression model for binary classification. We use stemming and stopword removal to clean our text and then use tf-idf to obtain numerical features that are then fed to the logistic regression model.

4.2. Support Vector Machine (SVM)

Another traditional machine learning method we use was a support vector machine (SVM), as they tend to work well in classification tasks (Meyer et al., 2003). For this method we use the same preprocessing as with the logistic regression model. The only difference being that we feed the tf-idf features to an SVM with a linear kernel rather than to a logistic regression model.

4.3. biLSTM

One of our neural models was a bidirectional LSTM. These are neural networks that use two LSTM (Hochreiter and Schmidhuber, 1997) layers, one in each direction, and then concatenate the hidden states of each direction to feed them to a linear layer for classification. For this model, we use only the first 300 tokens of each article in order to avoid disappearing gradients. We also use word2vec (Mikolov et al., 2013a; Mikolov et al., 2013b) in order to obtain intermediate representations of the text. More specifically, we use the Swedish embeddings trained on the CoNLL17 corpus[4] (Zeman et al., 2017) found at the NLPL word embeddings repository[5] (Fares et al., 2017).

4.4. BERT

The other neural model that we use is the Swedish verison of BERT released by the National Library of Sweden (Malmsten et al., 2020), available in the Hugging Face repository[6]. The first token of BERT's output, *[CLS]*, is then fed to a linear layer for classification.

In terms of specific implementation, we fine-tune the BERT model using our training data to obtain better representation of the text using this special token. We also use only the first 300 tokens of the text of each article to maintain consistency across the two neural models. Moreover, we use the BERT tokenizer in order to preprocess the text.

5. Experimental Results

Somewhat surprisingly, the logistic regression model outperformed all the others. Even though the one trained on the original training set fared poorly, when using EDA and subsampling the performance soars, achieving a F1-score of 0.759 on the unreliable articles and an overall F1-score of 0.866. This greatly outperforms the second best model, which is BERT using both EDA and subsampling with an F1-score of 0.709 for the unreliable for the unreliable articles and an overal F1-score of 0.837. The full results of our experiments can be seen in table 4 and are reported in terms of test set accuracy and F1-scores for the test set and for each class.

Regarding the traditional machine learning models, we can observe that with the logistic regression models any kind of augmentation improves the results. Meanwhile, EDA has a marked improvement for the SVM. Similarly, using subsampling improves both the overall F1-score and the F1-score for the unreliable class, even though we obtain a slightly worse F1-score for the reliable one.

With the LSTM models, we clearly note that subsampling leads to a worse perfomance of the models. Moreover, while we get mixed results with EDA, the F1-scores both overall and of the unreliable class are higher when using the unaltered training set. This is most likely due to having a small dataset to begin with, an issue made worse due to the data-hungry nature of LSTMs.

Finally, our BERT model performed the best when using EDA and subsampling.

6. Discussion

As mentioned before, we found it somewhat surprising that the best performing model was a variation of the baseline one. However, when looking at the representations we used, as well as how EDA works, it starts making more sense.

The idea of EDA is that we generate datapoints from random changes in the text. Even though in paper this is a good idea, it can have a noticeable impact on the more complex methods. For example, random swapping of words will wreck havoc in a sequential model such as LSTMs, while random swapping and insertion of synonyms can change the BERT models in unexpected ways. However, it is important to note that the BERT models that we used are pre-trained, so they can also better harness synonyms and similar changes.

On the other hand, tf-idf is a bag-of-words approach. This means that random insertions and swaps do not affect it at all. On the other hand, both backtranslation and synonym replacement should enhance the representations obtained through this method. Despite this, we wouldn't expect such improved results when compared to the neural network approaches.

It is important to note that the original EDA paper uses data from Twitter, which is limited to 140 characters. Even if we cropped the text of the articles to this length, the differences in information density would probably mean that the results would probably not be as good

[4]http://universaldependencies.org/conll17/

[5]http://vectors.nlpl.eu/repository/

[6]https://huggingface.co/KB/bert-base-swedish-cased

Model	Balanced	EDA	Acc.	F1-score overall	reliable	unreliable
LogReg	No	No	0.922	0.631	0.959	0.303
LogReg	No	Yes	0.943	0.767	0.969	0.564
LogReg	Yes	No	0.926	0.822	0.958	0.686
LogReg	**Yes**	**Yes**	**0.953**	**0.866**	**0.974**	**0.759**
SVM	No	No	0.949	0.803	0.973	0.634
SVM	No	Yes	**0.956**	**0.837**	**0.976**	**0.698**
SVM	Yes	No	0.929	0.828	0.960	0.696
SVM	Yes	Yes	0.929	0.828	0.960	0.696
LSTM	No	No	**0.943**	**0.824**	**0.968**	**0.679**
LSTM	No	Yes	0.939	0.810	0.967	0.654
LSTM	Yes	No	0.912	0.772	0.951	0.594
LSTM	Yes	Yes	0.885	0.731	0.935	0.528
LSTM + sent.	No	No	0.905	**0.755**	0.947	**0.563**
LSTM + sent.	No	Yes	**0.912**	0.752	**0.951**	0.552
LSTM + sent.	Yes	No	0.892	0.712	0.940	0.484
LSTM + sent.	Yes	Yes	0.889	0.715	0.937	0.492
BERT	No	No	0.939	0.746	0.968	0.679
BERT	No	Yes	0.945	0.785	**0.971**	0.600
BERT	Yes	Yes	**0.952**	**0.837**	0.966	**0.709**

Table 4: Result from evaluating the models on the test set. We report test set accuracy and F1-score for the full test set as well as for each class. For each kind of model we bolden the best result for the scores we report.

as with text that is naturally shorter. An interesting follow-up would be to test the effectiveness of EDA on datasets with lengthier tests to see whether there is any improvement in the results. It would also be interesting to change the implementation of EDA such that it is applied to each sentence in the input text independently rather than to the full input text.

Another possible follow-up experiment would be to use linguistic features rather than whole-document representations. This has proven to be a successful approach both with larger datasets (Horne et al., 2019) as well as with smaller ones (Pérez-Rosas et al., 2018). Moreover, a deeper error analysis could be done on these models.

7. Conclusions

Even though most studies on misinformation have focused on the English language, it is important to also study what happens in other languages. Different cultures react differently to global events and it is important to recognize that.

One of the main challenges we faced was a lack of annotated data on which to train our models. As far as we know, the only existing dataset so far is the one we used, introduced by Kokkinakis (2021). Even though news from unreliable sources are overtly abundant on social media and the rest of the web, it can be expensive or time-consuming to identify and label them. Moreover, Juneström (2021) note that the best known fact-checking website for Swedish news is no longer updated as of 2019. This makes it harder to gather fact-checked data on the COVID-19 pandemic in Sweden, both if we were to use annotations at source or at article levels.

In order to gather our own data, we would require the help from health and disinformation experts that are fluent in the language

We also realized that the use of EDA lead to surprisingly good results when using simple machine learning methods, especially when compared to deep learning approaches. As noted during the discussion, this might be due to the nature of the representations used for these models. These greater gains when comparing the two kinds of approaches might point out at EDA working better with either shorter texts or with non-serialized data.

It is only through assured access to the most updated information about the COVID-19 pandemic that we will be able to go through it sooner rather than later. The increasing spread of misinformation render healthcare measures less effective, allowing the virus to spread more widely.

8. Bibliographical References

Adhanom Ghebreyesus, T. (2020). Munich security conference. https://www.who.int/director-general/speeches/detail/munich-security-conference. World Health Organization. [Online; accessed 15-January-2022].

Baer, S. K. (2021). Thousands of anti-vax protesters marched in europe even though COVID deaths are rising. https://www.buzzfeednews.com/article/skbaer/antivax-europe-covid-mandates. BuzzFeed News. [Online; accessed 15-January-2022].

Derczynski, L., Bontcheva, K., Liakata, M., Procter, R., Wong Sak Hoi, G., and Zubiaga, A. (2017). SemEval-2017 task 8: RumourEval: Determining rumour veracity and support for rumours. In *Proceedings of the 11th International Workshop on Semantic Evaluation (SemEval-2017)*. Association for Computational Linguistics.

Edunov, S., Ott, M., Auli, M., and Grangier, D. (2018). Understanding back-translation at scale. In *Proceedings of the 2018 Conference on Empirical Methods in Natural Language Processing*. Association for Computational Linguistics.

Glad, E. and Sundberg, S. (2021). Tusenmannamarschen och coronaförnekandet. https://sverigesradio.se/avsnitt/1701155. In *P3 Nyheter Dokumentär*. Sveriges Radio [Online; accessed 16-January-2022].

Hochreiter, S. and Schmidhuber, J. (1997). Long short-term memory. In *Neural Computation*, volume 9, pages 1735–1780.

Horne, B. D., Nørregaard, J., and Adali, S. (2019). Robust fake news detection over time and attack. *ACM Transactions on Intelligent Systems and Technology*, 11(1):7:1–7:23.

Juneström, A. (2021). Discourses of fact-checking in swedish news media. *Journal of Documentation*, 78(7):125–140. Publisher: Emerald Publishing Limited.

Ma, J., Gao, W., and Wong, K.-F. (2018). Rumor detection on twitter with tree-structured recursive neural networks. In *Proceedings of the 56th Annual Meeting of the Association for Computational Linguistics (Volume 1: Long Papers)*. Association for Computational Linguistics.

Meyer, D., Leisch, F., and Hornik, K. (2003). The support vector machine under test. In *Neurocomputing*, volume 55, pages 169–186.

Mikolov, T., Chen, K., Corrado, G., and Dean, J. (2013a). Efficient estimation of word representations in vector space. *Arxiv preprint*. arXiv:1301.3781 [cs].

Mikolov, T., Sutskever, I., Chen, K., Corrado, G., and Dean, J. (2013b). Distributed representations of words and phrases and their compositionality. In *Proceedings of the 26th International Conference on Neural Information Processing Systems - Volume 2*, NIPS'13, pages 3111–3119. Curran Associates Inc.

Ortega, P. A., Maini, V., and DeepMind Safety Team. (2018). Building safe artificial intelligence: specification, robustness, and assurance. https://deepmindsafetyresearch.medium.com/building-safe-artificial-intelligence-52f5f75058f1. Medium [Online; accessed 14-January-2022].

Oshikawa, R., Qian, J., and Wang, W. Y. (2020). A survey on natural language processing for fake news detection. In *Proceedings of the 12th Language Resources and Evaluation Conference*. European Language Resources Association.

Pérez-Rosas, V., Kleinberg, B., Lefevre, A., and Mihalcea, R. (2018). Automatic detection of fake news. In *Proceedings of the 27th International Conference on Computational Linguistics*, pages 3391–3401. Association for Computational Linguistics.

Raza, S. (2021). Automatic fake news detection in political platforms - a transformer-based approach. In *Proceedings of the 4th Workshop on Challenges and Applications of Automated Extraction of Socio-political Events from Text (CASE 2021)*. Association for Computational Linguistics.

Shu, K., Mahudeswaran, D., Wang, S., Lee, D., and Liu, H. (2020). FakeNewsNet: A data repository with news content, social context, and spatiotemporal information for studying fake news on social media. In *Big Data*, volume 8, pages 171–188. Mary Ann Liebert, Inc.

Torabi Asr, F. and Taboada, M. (2018). The data challenge in misinformation detection: Source reputation vs. content veracity. In *Proceedings of the First Workshop on Fact Extraction and VERification (FEVER)*, pages 10–15. Association for Computational Linguistics.

Vijjali, R., Potluri, P., Kumar, S., and Teki, S. (2020). Two stage transformer model for COVID-19 fake news detection and fact checking. In *Proceedings of the 3rd NLP4IF Workshop on NLP for Internet Freedom: Censorship, Disinformation, and Propaganda*. International Committee on Computational Linguistics (ICCL).

Wei, J. and Zou, K. (2019). EDA: Easy data augmentation techniques for boosting performance on text classification tasks. In *Proceedings of the 2019 Conference on Empirical Methods in Natural Language Processing and the 9th International Joint Conference on Natural Language Processing (EMNLP-IJCNLP)*, pages 6382–6388. Association for Computational Linguistics.

Wikipedia. (2022). Protests over responses to the covid-19 pandemic — Wikipedia, the free encyclopedia. https://en.wikipedia.org/w/index.php?title=Protests_over_responses_to_the_COVID-19_pandemic. [Online; accessed 14-January-2022].

Zhou, X., Elfardy, H., Christodoulopoulos, C., Butler, T., and Bansal, M. (2021). Hidden biases in unreliable news detection datasets. In *Proceedings of the 16th Conference of the European Chapter of the Association for Computational Linguistics: Main Volume*. Association for Computational Linguistics.

9. Language Resource References

Borin, L., Forsberg, M., and Roxendal, J. (2012). Korp — the corpus infrastructure of språkbanken. In *Proceedings of the Eighth International Conference on Language Resources and Evaluation (LREC'12)*. European Language Resources Association (ELRA).

Fares, M., Kutuzov, A., Oepen, S., and Velldal, E. (2017). Word vectors, reuse, and replicability: Towards a community repository of large-text resources. In *Proceedings of the 21st Nordic Conference on Computational Linguistics, NoDaL-iDa*, Linköping Electronic Conference Proceedings. Linköping University Electronic Press, Linköpings universitet.

Kokkinakis, D. (2021). Insights on a swedish covid-19 corpus. In Monica Monachini et al., editors, *Proceedings of the CLARIN Annual Conference 2021*, pages 31–34.

Malmsten, M., Börjeson, L., and Haffenden, C. (2020). Playing with words at the national library of sweden – making a swedish BERT. *Arxiv preprint*. arXiv:2007.01658 [cs].

Zeman, D., Popel, M., Straka, M., Hajič, J., Nivre, J., Ginter, F., Luotolahti, J., Pyysalo, S., Petrov, S., Potthast, M., Tyers, F., Badmaeva, E., Gokirmak, M., Nedoluzhko, A., Cinková, S., Hajič jr., J., Hlaváčová, J., Kettnerová, V., Urešová, Z., Kanerva, J., Ojala, S., Missilä, A., Manning, C. D., Schuster, S., Reddy, S., Taji, D., Habash, N., Leung, H., de Marneffe, M.-C., Sanguinetti, M., Simi, M., Kanayama, H., de Paiva, V., Droganova, K., Martínez Alonso, H., Çöltekin, C., Sulubacak, U., Uszkoreit, H., Macketanz, V., Burchardt, A., Harris, K., Marheinecke, K., Rehm, G., Kayadelen, T., Attia, M., Elkahky, A., Yu, Z., Pitler, E., Lertpradit, S., Mandl, M., Kirchner, J., Alcalde, H. F., Strnadová, J., Banerjee, E., Manurung, R., Stella, A., Shimada, A., Kwak, S., Mendonça, G., Lando, T., Nitisaroj, R., and Li, J. (2017). CoNLL 2017 shared task: Multilingual parsing from raw text to universal dependencies. In *Proceedings of the CoNLL 2017 Shared Task: Multilingual Parsing from Raw Text to Universal Dependencies*. Association for Computational Linguistics.

Proceedings of the ResT-UP2 Proceedings @LREC2022, pages 8–15
Marseille, 20-25 June 2022

BanglaHateBERT: BERT for Abusive Language Detection in Bengali

Md Saroar Jahan[⋆], **Mainul Haque** [◇], **Nabil Arhab** [⋆], **Mourad Oussalah**[⋆]
[⋆]University of Oulu, CMVS, BP 4500, 90014, Finland
[◇] City University, Dhaka, Bangladesh
{Md.Jahan,Nabil.Arhab, Mourad.Oussalah}@oulu.fi, mainul37@gmail.com

Abstract

This paper introduces BanglaHateBERT, a retrained BERT model for abusive language detection in Bengali. The model was trained with a large-scale Bengali offensive, abusive, and hateful corpus that we have collected from different sources and made available to the public. Furthermore, we have collected and manually annotated 15K Bengali hate speech balanced dataset and made it publicly available for the research community. We used existing pre-trained BanglaBERT model and retrained it with 1.5 million offensive posts. We presented the results of a detailed comparison between generic pre-trained language model and retrained with the abuse-inclined version. In all datasets, BanglaHateBERT outperformed the corresponding available BERT model.

Keywords: Bangla Hate BERT, Bangla Hate Dataset

1. Introduction

Bengali (pronunciation: [baŋla]) is the 6th most spoken language worldwide, spoken by almost 260 million people, offering resources for potential hate speech detection. The Bengali language is Bangladesh's national language and the second most-spoken language in India (Thompson, 2012). The development of the internet in society promoted the freedom of speech at an unprecedented level. This has led to a continuous rise of hate speech and offensive language on social media. For instance, online abuse towards females is continuously rising in Bangladesh (Sambasivan et al., 2019). In addition, the development of machine learning models to tackle hate speech in real-time is challenging for low resource languages like Bengali because of a lack of datasets and tools for Bengali text classification (Hussain et al., 2018). Only a few works have been reported on Bengali hate speech detection in social media. For instance, we found the claim of six Bengali hate speech datasets and research work. However, only two datasets are publicly available. Among by (Karim et al., 2020), which is annotated into five different classes and follows the native Bengali dialect. Nevertheless, this dataset does not contain any non-hate classes that might fall short during model training for hate and non-hate detection. Another dataset by (Awal et al., 2018) of 2665 sentences translated from an English hate speech dataset that lacks the dialect of native Bengali. Furthermore, some datasets were code-mixed and written in English (Banik and Rahman, 2019). Besides, none of the datasets are balanced in terms of their classes, and only a tiny percentage contained hate samples (Romim et al., 2021). Table 1 shows a comparison of state-of-the-art datasets on Bengali hate speech.

We can distinguish three categories of automatic abusive language detection using natural language processing (NLP) pipeline: i) feature-based linear classifiers (Waseem and Hovy, 2016), (Ribeiro et al., 2018), ii) neural network architectures (e.g., CNN or Bi-LSTM) (Kshirsagar et al., 2018), (Mishra et al., 2018), (Mitrović et al., 2019), and, finally, iii) fine-tuning pre-trained language models, e.g., BERT, RoBERTa, (Liu et al., 2019), (Swamy et al., 2019). Results vary both across datasets and architectures, where linear classifiers showed good training performance but lower accuracy scores compared to neural architecture or BERT-like models. On the other hand, systems using pre-trained language models have gained momentum in the field. Although a common problem with pre-trained models is that the training language combination makes them well-fitted for general-purpose language understanding tasks, but their limits are well-acknowledged when facing domain-specific language tasks. To address this limitation, there is a growing interest in developing domain-specific BERT-like pre-trained language models, such as AlBERTo (Polignano et al., 2019) or TweetEval (Barbieri et al., 2020) for Twitter dataset, BioBERT for biomedical domain in English (Lee et al., 2020), FinBERT for the financial domain in English (Yang et al., 2020), IndicBERT (BERT for major Indian language (Kakwani et al., 2020)), LEGAL-BERT for the legal domain in English (Chalkidis et al., 2020) and HateBERT (BERT for English Hate speech) (Caselli et al., 2020). Similarly, for Bengali text classification, BnglaBERT (Sarker, 2021) has been promoted and shown to outperform other BERT models (i.e., indicBERT, m-BERT). However, this model was trained with general Bengali text and does not contain much hate text, which falls short in hate speech classification tasks. To enrich this model, we introduce BanglaHateBERT, a pre-trained BERT model for abusive language phenomena in social media in Bengali. Besides, since abusive language phenomena covers a wide spectrum, e.g., microaggression, stereotyping, offense, abuse, hate speech, threats, and doxing (Jurgens et al., 2019), our BenglaHateBERT contributes to identifying a wide range of Bengali abusive text.

This aims to bridge the gap in availability of the Ben-

Table 1: A comparison of all state of the art datasets on Bengali hate speech

Paper	Total data	Number Of class	Language	Availability
Classification Benchmarks for Under-resourced Bengali Language based on Multichannel Convolutional-LSTM Network (Karim et al., 2020)	5,699	05	Native Bengali	Publicly available
Hateful speech detection in public Facebook pages for the Bengali language (Ishmam and Sharmin, 2019)	5,126	06	Native Bengali	Not available
Toxicity Detection on Bengali Social Media Comments using Supervised Models (Banik and Rahman, 2019)	10,219	05	Mixed Bengali English	No available
A Deep Learning Approach to Detect Abusive Bengali Text (Emon et al., 2019)	4,700	07	Native Bengali	Not available
Threat and Abusive Language Detection on Social Media in Bengali Language (Chakraborty and Seddiqui, 2019)	5,644	07	Native Bengali	Not available
Detecting Abusive Comments in Discussion Threads Using Naïve Bayes (Awal et al., 2018)	2,665	07	Translated English to Bengali	Publicly available
Hate Speech detection in the Bengali language: A dataset and its baseline evaluation (Romim et al., 2021)	30,000	02	Native Bengali	Not available

gali hate dataset and pre-trained BERT model for Bengali domain-specific abusive language detection. Overall, this paper claims threefold contributions as follows:

1. A new 1540k Bengali offensive corpus collected from Reddit-banned offensive comments is released.

2. A new 15k native Bengali offensive balanced corpus and manually labeled as offensive and non-offensive, collected from youtube, and Facebook users' comments, is made available.

3. We proposed a domain-specific pre-trained BERT model, referred BanglaHateBERT, for the purpose of Bengali offensive/hate speech detection.

Section 2 describes the dataset development process, including corpus statistics, hate categories identification, annotator and annotation guidelines, and disagreement handling. Section 3 illustrates the BanglaHateBERT construction, including a brief introduction of BERT. The results are provided in Section 4.2 and finally, Section 5 draws the main findings of this work.

2. Creation of Bengali Hate Dataset

We shall consider a new Bengali dataset for textual offensive speech annotated at the sentence level. To collect data, we used the beautiful-soup[1] python library to directly collect data and convert them into CSV file format. We collected data from Facebook and Youtube mainly from social media groups, celebrity pages, local Bengali news pages, political news posts, roasting videos, and funny content posts from 1 January 2021 to 05 April 2022. First, we collected 110k posts and then filtered 8.5k with Bengali profane word string matching to increase the chances of hitting offensive posts (examples of profane words shown in Table 3). At the same time, for the purpose of enforcing class balance, we also identified 8.5k posts from the original dataset that do not contain offensive/hate content. Finally, we manually label these total of 17k offensive and non-offensive posts, and after data preprocessing and manual scrutinizing, we kept 15k that held up to our standard by discarding noise comments or statements presenting only Bengali text. In other words, we mainly remove unidentified characters, symbols, numbers, mentioned tags, emojis, tab tokens, URLs, etc. We have not performed the removal of stop-words and stemming for preserving data quality. The statistics of the collected dataset are summarized in Table 2.
Next, to identify hate-speech content from the collected dataset, we first highlight the categories of hate speech that are investigated in the subsequent analysis. This is detailed in the next subsection.

2.1. Hate categories identification

Hate speech often occurs with different linguistic connotations, even in subtle forms (Fortuna and Nunes, 2018). Due to the nature of its diversity, we identified eight hate speech targets, which we describe and

[1]https://www.crummy.com/software/BeautifulSoup/bs4/doc/

Table 2: Statistic of Dataset.

Statistics	**Count**
Number of Tokens	190,823
Vocabulary Size	26430
Number of Posts	15000
Average number of Tokens per post	12.7
Non-hate class	7500
Hate class	7500

provide examples from the corpus as follows:

Xenophobia: is a term that primarily represents the form of discrimination manifested through biased actions and hate against foreigners (DE OLIVEIRA, 2020). An example: 'রোহিঙ্গারা আসার পর ইয়াবা ব্যাবসা অনেক বেড়ে গেছে। ' - 'After the arrival of Rohingyas, there was increased Yaba drug business'.

Racism: racism or racial segregation consists of a tendency of racial domination (Wolfe, 1999). (Clair and Denis, 2015) pointed out that racism is a biological or a cultural dominance of one or more racial groups related to, e.g., skin color or physical look differences. For example, from the corpus: 'রোহিঙ্গারা সব হারামি, ওদের দেশে না রাখাই ভালো ' -Rohingyas are all bastards, it is better not to keep them in the country'.

Sexual: This includes expressions with a sexual meaning or intention. Examples from the corpus is: 'আর আমি, বাড়া দিলে তুমি স-যত্নে গ্রহণ করিতে মনজিলে মাকসুদের পানি শুকিয়ে প্লাস্টিকের অর্গানিক বাঁড়া চাইতে!'-'And me, give you my d**k, you would take care of it, dry the water in the floor and ask for organic d**k!'. However, innocent sexual talk and sex educational conversions are considered differently (e.g., 'হস্তমৈথুন ভাল বা খারাপ ?'- 'Masturbation good or bad?').

Religious fundamentalism/Religious Intolerance: This is consistently associated with high levels of intolerance and prejudices toward targeting specific religious groups (Altemeyer and Altemeyer, 1996). This is exemplified in the following post: 'হিন্দুরা শিশ্ন পূজা করে'-'Hindu people worship dick'.

Homophobia: This corresponds to negative attitudes and feelings toward homosexuality. This includes people who are identified or perceived as being lesbian, gay, and bisexual. An example of this case from our corpus is: 'সালা সমকামী, পিছন দিয়ে করে '-'He is gay, he get f**k in his back'.

Besides the above-mentioned categories, we have also considered hate toward a person, geopolitical or political organization. For example, 'বিএনপির ঘরে ধুকে একটা একটা করে মারবো'-'We will target and kill each BNP by entering their house', this is a severe threat towards a political party which does not fall into the above categories; however, it fulfills the definition of hate speech. In the next section, we describe the process of manual annotation, indicating how a given post lies within a specific category of hate speech.

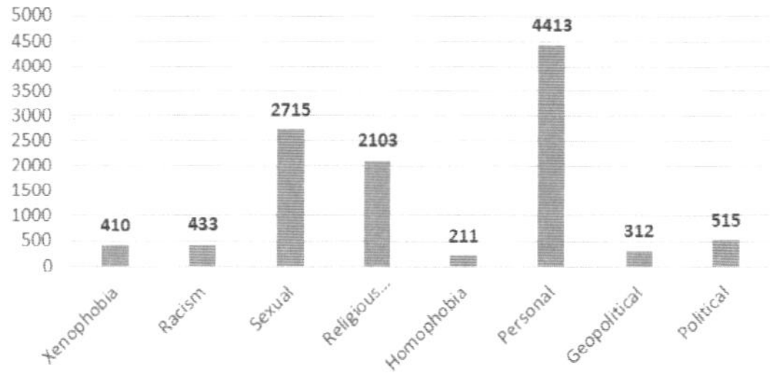

Figure 1: The number of hate samples in each category (same sample can exist in multiple categories).

2.2. Annotation Guidelines

The annotation involves identifying whether each sentence contains a hate speech or not by following the previously described hate categorization. In this study, all the annotators created and discussed the guidelines to ensure all participants had the same understanding of hate speech. A total of 27 independent native Bengali labelers have been employed separately to avoid bias. All annotators hold a minimum of a Bachelor's degree or are final-year Bachelor's students with a full ability to understand annotation guidelines. Besides, a research fellow has resolved disagreements between more than two annotators, who is a Ph.D. candidate in this field, and was called whenever a disagreement arises (total disagreement 339). If a sentence includes a hate, regardless of its hate category, it is given the label '1'; otherwise, it is assigned '0'. See examples shown in Table 4.

In our annotation, a sentence is considered *hate* if it satisfies the following criteria drawn from the hate definition by (Brown, 2017; Anis and Maret, 2017; Chetty and Alathur, 2018): *deliberate attack directed towards a specific group of people or organization employing sexual attack, curse, defamation, threat, gender, ethnicity, and identity.* Similar guidelines are also followed by Facebook and the youtube community for considering hate speech, which states *'Hate speech is a sentence that dehumanizes one or multiple persons or a community'*. Dehumanizing can be done by comparing the person or community to an insect, object, or criminal. It can also be done by targeting a person based on their race, gender, physical and mental disability [2]. A sentence might contain slang or inappropriate language. But unless that slang dehumanizes a person or community, we did not consider it to be associated with a hate speech [3]. Indeed, the presence or absence of offensive/abusive/profane words in a sentence cannot systematically be considered an acceptable proof to establish the existence of hate or not-hate. For example, Sentence 3 ('Gf why your two things are big') from Table-1 does not contain any offensive word, though, by definition, it is very offensive to someone. Another example in Sentence 4 ('some

[2] https://web.facebook.com/communitystandards/

[3] https://www.youtube.com/howyoutubeworks/policies/community-guidelines/

Table 3: Example of profane words.

Type	Words	English Trsnlation
Offensive	চুদি	F**k
Offensive	মাগী	Bi*ch
Offensive	সমকামী	Gay
Offensive	কাইলা	Black(skin color)
Offensive	খানকির পোলা	Bastard
Swear words	জাহান্নামে যাবি	Go to Hell
Swear words	মাইরা ফেলমু	kill you

people are just bastards, just ignore them'), includes the profane word 'Bastards'; however, it does not target any specific group; rather, it might have supported the victim, which makes it a non-hate sentence. Therefore, with regards to hate speech (HS), we decided to consider two characteristics for its identification:

1. There must be a target (i.e., an individual, race/group/community, or an organization), and
2. The action, or intention of the statement (Searle and Searle, 1969): this means that we must deal with a message that incites, spreads, promotes, or support violence or hatred towards the given target or a statement that aims at dehumanizing, delegitimizing, hurting or intimidating the target.

To understand the action or intention of the speaker, the use of profane words plays an important role. This is defined as socially improper use of language that includes offensive, cursing, swearing, or expletive wording. Table 3 highlights examples of frequent profane words extracted from the corpus.
Once labeled, 50% (7.5k) of the dataset was identified as hate, while the rest 50% (7.5k) were non-hate sentences. The final version of the dataset is saved in a CSV file that contains three columns (Posts: refer to collected sentences; Label: the judgment of the annotator in terms of hate or non-hate; Category: the type of hate speech). The details of the dataset collection are made available at this GitHub page[4].

2.3. Inter Annotator Agreement

We used Krippendorff's alpha (α) (Krippendorff, 1970) to measure the inter-annotator agreement because of the nature of our annotation setup. This robust statistical measure accounts for possible incomplete data and, therefore, does not require every annotator to annotate every sentence systematically.

$$\alpha = 1 - \frac{D_o}{D_e} \tag{1}$$

Here α is calculated by Equation (1), where (D_o) is the observed number of disagreements and (D_e) stands for the estimated likelihood of a disagreement occurring.

[4]https://github.com/saroarjahan/BanglaHateBert

We used nominal metrics to calculate annotator agreement. The range of α is between 0 and 1, 1 α 0. When α = 1, there is perfect agreement between annotators, and when α=0, the agreement is entirely due to a chance. Our annotation produced an agreement reliability score of 0.919 using nominal metric .

Disagreement Cases:
Our inter-annotator agreement score was satisfactory (α = 0.913); however, some minor disagreements occurred. Below we summarize some problematic annotating examples that raise conflict among annotators.

1. 'দিঘী এখন সাগর হয় গেছে' - Dighi has now become the sea': Not sure whether the speaker used word 'sea' in a vulgar way in Bengali targeting a Bangladeshi actress 'Dighi'.
2. 'ব্যশ্যাস্যালয়ের মাটি ছাড়া দূর্গা মূর্তি গড়া অসম্পূর্ণ!' - 'It is incomplete to build a Durga idol without the soil of the brothel! ': Not sure whether the speaker intends to provide information or to devalue targeting the Hindu religion.
3. 'তাহসানের বউ এখন আরেকজনের বৌ' - 'Tahsan's wife is now someone else's wife': This post doesn't consist of any hate/swear words; however, mentioning someone's 'wife' might have the intention of defamation or insult or no intention at all. Therefore, it was complex to comprehend the intention of the speaker.
4. 'তুমি তো বরিশাইল্যা'-' You are Barisallya': The word 'Barishallya' is an ethnic slur typically used refers to a particular people of a region. Sometimes this is used as an insult and sometimes as a fun connotation.
5. 'ওরাল সেক্স কি করা যাবে'-'Can we do oral sex?': Despite the fact that this sample contains offensive terms, the speaker's goal may be harmless, and the question may be asked for educational purposes.

3. Creation of BanglaHateBERT

The Bidirectional Encoder Representations from Transformers (BERT) is a seminal transformer-based language model that involves an attention mechanism that enables contextual learning relations between words in a text sequence (Devlin et al., 2018). Two training strategies were used in our BERT model:

1. Masked-Language Modeling (MLM): where 15 % of the tokens in a sequence are masked, and then the model learns to predict those tokens.
2. Next sentence prediction (NSP): here, the model accepts two sentences as input and learns whether the second sentence is a successor of the first sentence in their original document context.

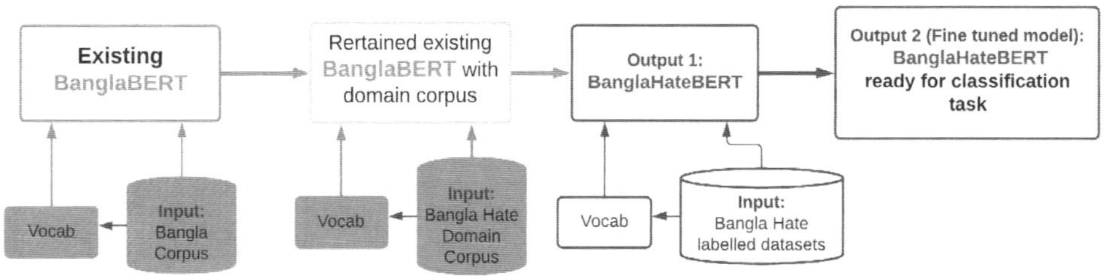

Figure 2: The architecture of BanglaHateBERT (Output1), can be used for further training with labeled corpus and ready for text classification tasks.

Sentence	Translation	Label	Categories
1. ওমি একটা পাগলা হালায় আছিলো।মাথায় গু আছিলো হালার	Omi is a crazzy, head full off shit	1	Personal
2. যেগুলো মানুষের নিত্যপ্রয়োজনীয় সেই গুলো দাম বাড়ছে। এই বাজেট কোনভাবে জনহিতকর বাজেট হতে পারে না	The prices of the necessities of life are rising. This budget can in no way be a public interest budget.	0	-
3. বান্ধবী তোমার ও দুটো এতো বড় কেনো	Gf why your two things is big	1	Personal, Sexual
4. কিছু মানুষ এমনিতেই হারামি এদের এত পাত্তা দিয়েন না	some people are just bastards just ignore them	0	-
5. তোদের মত নাস্তিকের বাচ্চার জন্য মুসলমানদের আজকের বদনাম	Today's notoriety of Muslims for the child of an atheist like you	1	Religious
6. ১৯৭১ এ ভারতের সাহায্য না করলে আজ পাকিস্তানের পা চাটতে	If India had not helped in 1971, Pakistan would have been licked today	1	Geoplitical
7. তুইতো একটা রেইনবো	Your are a rainbow (meaing gay)	1	Personal, Homophobia

Table 4: Annotation examples from original dataset with English translation. Label 1 refers to hate, and 0 refers to non-hate, categories column refers to type of hate speech.

The creation of BanglaHateBERT follows a two-step process is highlighted in Figure 3. First, we collected the large-scale Bangla offensive corpus, and then we retrained the existing BnaglaBERT with this Bengali offensive corpus.

Large-scale Bengali offensive corpus: Because of the lack of large-scale Bengali hate corpus for BERT training, we initially translated 16 offensive English hate datasets, with a total of 157k offensive sentences[5] to Bengali using Google API[6]. Furthermore, we have collected and translated (English to Bengali) 1478k Reddit-banned sentences that were considered offensive posts by the Reddit community. Finally, we have used these offensive sentences to retrain the BERT model.

Large scale Bengali pre-trained BERT model: To retrain the BERT model, we used an existing BanglaBERT model, a Bangla language model trained on 18.6 GB of Internet-crawled data from Wikipedia Bangla pages. In other words, the BanglaBERT model is trained on 1 million training steps over 3 billion tokens (24B characters) of Bengali text drawn from news, online discussion, and internet crawl (Sarker, 2021).

[5]https://hatespeechdata.com/

[6]https://pypi.org/project/googletrans/

From the offensive corpus, we used 1,635,348 messages (a total of 40,309,341 tokens) to retrain the BanglaBERT base-uncased model by applying the Masked Language Model (MLM). We retrained for 15 epochs (almost 2 million steps) in batches of 64 samples, including up to 512 sentence tokens. We used Adam with a learning rate of 5e-5, which is an optimization solver for the Neural Network algorithm that is computationally efficient and requires little memory (Kingma and Ba, 2014). We trained using the huggingface code on one NvidiaRTX 3070 GPU. The result is a shifted BanglaBERT model to BanglaHateBERT.

4. Evaluation of BanglaHateBERT

To verify the validity and suitability of BanglaHateBERT, we compared it with other popular BERT models related to Bengali (i.e., BanglaBERT, multilingual-BERT, indicBERT). In addition, we also compared BERT performance with other deep-learning models CNN. We used one Bengali benchmarked dataset (Karim et al., 2020) for testing model performance. In contrast, we used our collected Bengali hate speech dataset as well.

Table 5: Performance comparison of BanglaHateBERT vs. other models in terms of classifier Accuracy (%) and F1 scores (%) for Bengali hate speech detection using(Karim et al., 2020) dataset. Best scores are in bold.

Classifier	Accuracy	F1
CNN + fastText	92.1	91.3
BERT-multilingual	80	79.4
IndicBERT	89.4	88.1
BanglaBERT	92.4	92
BanglaHateBERT	**93.1**	**92.8**

4.1. Classifier Architecture

We performed a binary hate speech classification. For consistency, we used the same training, validation, and test samples for all models. We randomly shuffled and divided the entire collected dataset into three parts: training, validation, and testing set. For both datasets, we have used 70% for training, 10% for validation, and 20% for testing the model.

CNN-fastText Model Structure: We adopted (Kim, 2014) CNN architecture, where the input layer is represented by a concatenation of the words forming the post (up to 70 words), except that each word is now represented by its fastText embedding representation with a 300 embedding vector. Word embedding maps each token to a vector of real numbers aiming to quantify and categorize the semantic similarities between linguistic terms based on their distributional properties in a large corpus using machine learning or related dimensional reduction techniques. We used the pre-trained word embeddings; namely, Bengali fastText [7]. A convolution 1D operation with a kernel size of 3 was used with a max-over-time pooling operation over the feature map with a layer dense 50. Dropout on the penultimate layer with a constraint on l2-norm of the weight vector was used for regularization.

BERT Model Structure: We used Huggingface Transformers (Wolf et al., 2019) library for implementing the classifiers. We fine-tuned different transformer training data using 70% training data. The following models were tested: BanglaBERT, IndicBERT(covering 12 major Indian languages, multilingual-BERT (mBERT uncased), and BanglaHateBERT. Each model was fine-tuned for 6 epochs with a learning rate of 5e-6, maximum input sequence length of 128, and batch size 4. After each epoch, the model was evaluated on the test set. Fig. 3 illustrates our BERT architecture

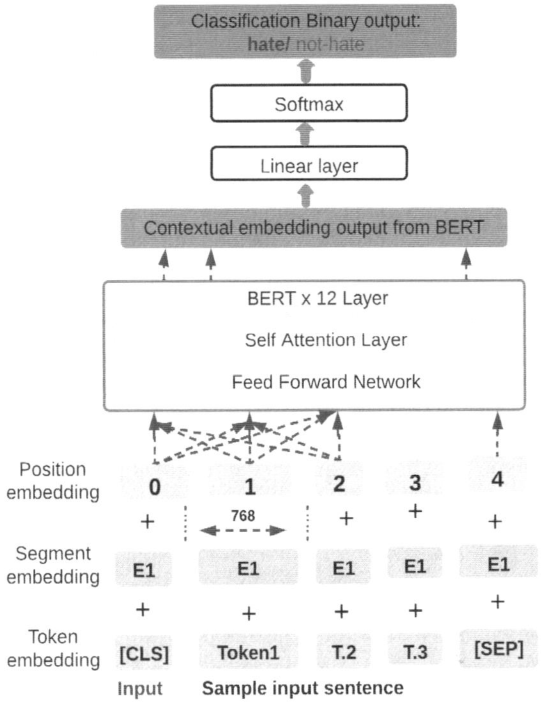

Figure 3: The general BERT architecture for text classification.

Table 6: Performance comparison of BanglaHateBERT Vs. other models in terms of hate speech classification Accuracy (%) and F1 scores (%) using our 15k balanced dataset. Best scores are in bold.

Classifier	Accuracy	F1
CNN + fastText	92.6	92.1
BERT-multilingual	82.1	81.3
IndicBERT	89.8	89.3
BanglaBERT	93.1	93
BanglaHateBERT	**94.3**	**94.1**

4.2. Results

The results of the binary classification of Bengali hate dataset by (Karim et al., 2020) and our collected dataset are summarized in Table 5, which shows classifier accuracy and F1 score for all four types of classifiers.

Among all five classifiers, BnaglaHateBERT outperformed all other models, indicating that the suggested BanglaHateBERT contextual model works better than the general one. These results have been observed for both balanced and unbalanced datasets, which followed an identical model performance rank: mBERT, IndicBERT, FastText, BanglaBERT, and BanglaHateBERT). For example, in both datasets, mBERT performed the lowest in terms of accuracy and F1 score compared to IndicBERT and BanglaBERT. This low

[7]https://fasttext.cc/docs/en/crawl-vectors.html (accessed 30.12.2021)

performance of mBERT can be explained by the fact that mBERThas was trained in over 102 languages. However, since it has only a small percentage of Bengali tokens, it falls short for domain-specific tasks. On the other hand, InbdicBERT performed overall better than mBERT, although it is also a multilingual BERT model. However, IndicBERT was trained over large-scale corpora covering 12 major Indian languages, containing a large portion of Bengali tokens (850 million). In both experiments, BnaglaBERT performed much better than mBERT and indicBERT since it has 3 billion Bengali tokens, which is much higher than mBERT and indicBERT. However, BanglaHateBERT performed even better than BanglaBERT since it has an additional 4 million tokens, which are primarily derived from the offensive corpus. The in-domain results confirm the validity of the re-training approach to generate better models for the detection of abusive language phenomena. On every dataset, BanglaHateBERT outperforms the corresponding general BERT model. These results can be further explained by observing the fastText model performance. For example, fastText did not perform better than BanglaBERT and BanglaHatebERT, which suggests that NLP contextual model is preferable compared to non-contextual word embeddings like fastText. However, interestingly it has outperformed indicBERT and mBERT as well, which indicates that the number of tokens highly influences model performance.

Strictly speaking, as far as we know, the (Karim et al., 2020) dataset has not been tested with BERT model previously. However, it has been tested with the deep learning model with word2vec embeddings and yielded 92.1% accuracy, which is 2% lower than our best performing model.

5. Conclusion

This paper introduced a new Bengali hate speech annotated dataset and BERT model for Bengali hate speech detection and experimented with mBERT, IndicBERT, BanglaBERT, and CNN models. To the best of our knowledge, this work is the first application of the BERT hate model trained with a domain-specific 1.5 million hate domain posts for Bengali. In addition, we published a balanced dataset (50% hate and 50% non-hate), which contains 15k posts collected from youtube and Facebook, which were then manually labeled and covered large categories of hate speech. In all cases, BanglaHateBERT has performed outstandingly in detecting hate speech compared to the mBERT, indicBERT, BanglaBERT, and CNN models, suggesting the effectiveness of domain-based contextual model performance over the non-domain-based contextual model. The developed BanglaHateBERT yields 94.3% accuracy and 94.1% F1 scores, which outperformed alternative models by a non-negligible margin.

6. Acknowledgements

This work is partially supported by EU YoungRes (ID. 823701) and Cost Action Nexus Linguarum, which are gratefully acknowledged.

7. Bibliographical References

Altemeyer, R. A. and Altemeyer, B. (1996). *The authoritarian specter*. Harvard University Press.

Anis, M. and Maret, U. (2017). Hatespeech in arabic language. In *International Conference on Media Studies*.

Awal, M. A., Rahman, M. S., and Rabbi, J. (2018). Detecting abusive comments in discussion threads using naïve bayes. In *2018 International Conference on Innovations in Science, Engineering and Technology (ICISET)*, pages 163–167. IEEE.

Banik, N. and Rahman, M. H. H. (2019). Toxicity detection on bengali social media comments using supervised models. In *2019 2nd International Conference on Innovation in Engineering and Technology (ICIET)*, pages 1–5. IEEE.

Barbieri, F., Camacho-Collados, J., Neves, L., and Espinosa-Anke, L. (2020). Tweeteval: Unified benchmark and comparative evaluation for tweet classification. *arXiv preprint arXiv:2010.12421*.

Brown, A. (2017). What is hate speech? part 1: The myth of hate. *Law and Philosophy*, 36(4):419–468.

Caselli, T., Basile, V., Mitrović, J., and Granitzer, M. (2020). Hatebert: Retraining bert for abusive language detection in english. *arXiv preprint arXiv:2010.12472*.

Chakraborty, P. and Seddiqui, M. H. (2019). Threat and abusive language detection on social media in bengali language. In *2019 1st International Conference on Advances in Science, Engineering and Robotics Technology (ICASERT)*, pages 1–6. IEEE.

Chalkidis, I., Fergadiotis, M., Malakasiotis, P., Aletras, N., and Androutsopoulos, I. (2020). Legal-bert: The muppets straight out of law school. *arXiv preprint arXiv:2010.02559*.

Chetty, N. and Alathur, S. (2018). Hate speech review in the context of online social networks. *Aggression and violent behavior*, 40:108–118.

Clair, M. and Denis, J. S. (2015). Sociology of racism. international encyclopedia of the social and behavioral sciences 2nd.

DE OLIVEIRA, L. M. (2020). Imigrantes, xenofobia e racismo: uma análise de conflitos em escolas municipais de são paulo.

Devlin, J., Chang, M.-W., Lee, K., and Toutanova, K. (2018). Bert: Pre-training of deep bidirectional transformers for language understanding. *arXiv preprint arXiv:1810.04805*.

Emon, E. A., Rahman, S., Banarjee, J., Das, A. K., and Mittra, T. (2019). A deep learning approach to detect abusive bengali text. In *2019 7th International Conference on Smart Computing & Communications (ICSCC)*, pages 1–5. IEEE.

Fortuna, P. and Nunes, S. (2018). A survey on automatic detection of hate speech in text. *ACM Computing Surveys (CSUR)*, 51(4):1–30.

Hussain, M. G., Al Mahmud, T., and Akthar, W. (2018). An approach to detect abusive bangla text. In *2018 International Conference on Innovation in Engineering and Technology (ICIET)*, pages 1–5. IEEE.

Ishmam, A. M. and Sharmin, S. (2019). Hateful speech detection in public facebook pages for the bengali language. In *2019 18th IEEE International Conference On Machine Learning And Applications (ICMLA)*, pages 555–560. IEEE.

Jurgens, D., Chandrasekharan, E., and Hemphill, L. (2019). A just and comprehensive strategy for using nlp to address online abuse. *arXiv preprint arXiv:1906.01738*.

Kakwani, D., Kunchukuttan, A., Golla, S., N.C., G., Bhattacharyya, A., Khapra, M. M., and Kumar, P. (2020). IndicNLPSuite: Monolingual Corpora, Evaluation Benchmarks and Pre-trained Multilingual Language Models for Indian Languages. In *Findings of EMNLP*.

Karim, M. R., Chakravarti, B. R., P. McCrae, J., and Cochez, M. (2020). Classification benchmarks for under-resourced bengali language based on multichannel convolutional-lstm network. In *7th IEEE International Conference on Data Science and Advanced Analytics (IEEE DSAA,2020)*. IEEE.

Kim, Y. (2014). Convolutional neural networks for sentence classification. *arXiv preprint arXiv:1408.5882*.

Kingma, D. P. and Ba, J. (2014). Adam: A method for stochastic optimization. *arXiv preprint arXiv:1412.6980*.

Krippendorff, K. (1970). Estimating the reliability, systematic error and random error of interval data. *Educational and Psychological Measurement*, 30(1):61–70.

Kshirsagar, R., Cukuvac, T., McKeown, K., and McGregor, S. (2018). Predictive embeddings for hate speech detection on twitter. *arXiv preprint arXiv:1809.10644*.

Lee, J., Yoon, W., Kim, S., Kim, D., Kim, S., So, C. H., and Kang, J. (2020). Biobert: a pre-trained biomedical language representation model for biomedical text mining. *Bioinformatics*, 36(4):1234–1240.

Liu, P., Li, W., and Zou, L. (2019). Nuli at semeval-2019 task 6: Transfer learning for offensive language detection using bidirectional transformers. In *SemEval@ NAACL-HLT*, pages 87–91.

Mishra, P., Yannakoudakis, H., and Shutova, E. (2018). Neural character-based composition models for abuse detection. *arXiv preprint arXiv:1809.00378*.

Mitrović, J., Birkeneder, B., and Granitzer, M. (2019). nlpup at semeval-2019 task 6: A deep neural language model for offensive language detection. In *Proceedings of the 13th International Workshop on Semantic Evaluation*, pages 722–726.

Polignano, M., Basile, P., De Gemmis, M., and Semeraro, G. (2019). Hate speech detection through alberto italian language understanding model. In *NL4AI@ AI* IA*, pages 1–13.

Ribeiro, M. H., Calais, P. H., Santos, Y. A., Almeida, V. A., and Meira Jr, W. (2018). Characterizing and detecting hateful users on twitter. In *Twelfth international AAAI conference on web and social media*.

Romim, N., Ahmed, M., Talukder, H., Islam, S., et al. (2021). Hate speech detection in the bengali language: A dataset and its baseline evaluation. In *Proceedings of International Joint Conference on Advances in Computational Intelligence*, pages 457–468. Springer.

Sambasivan, N., Batool, A., Ahmed, N., Matthews, T., Thomas, K., Gaytán-Lugo, L. S., Nemer, D., Bursztein, E., Churchill, E., and Consolvo, S. (2019). " they don't leave us alone anywhere we go" gender and digital abuse in south asia. In *proceedings of the 2019 CHI Conference on Human Factors in Computing Systems*, pages 1–14.

Sarker, S. (2021). Banglabert: Bengali mask language model for bengali language understanding.

Searle, J. R. and Searle, J. R. (1969). *Speech acts: An essay in the philosophy of language*, volume 626. Cambridge university press.

Swamy, S. D., Jamatia, A., and Gambäck, B. (2019). Studying generalisability across abusive language detection datasets. In *Proceedings of the 23rd conference on computational natural language learning (CoNLL)*, pages 940–950.

Thompson, H.-R. (2012). *Bengali*, volume 18. John Benjamins Publishing.

Waseem, Z. and Hovy, D. (2016). Hateful symbols or hateful people? predictive features for hate speech detection on twitter. In *Proceedings of the NAACL student research workshop*, pages 88–93.

Wolf, T., Debut, L., Sanh, V., Chaumond, J., Delangue, C., Moi, A., Cistac, P., Rault, T., Louf, R., Funtowicz, M., et al. (2019). Huggingface's transformers: State-of-the-art natural language processing. *arXiv preprint arXiv:1910.03771*.

Wolfe, A. (1999). The bridge over the racial divide: Rising inequality and coalition politics. *The Journal of Blacks in Higher Education*, (26):127.

Yang, Y., Uy, M. C. S., and Huang, A. (2020). Finbert: A pretrained language model for financial communications. *arXiv preprint arXiv:2006.08097*.

Proceedings of the ResT-UP2 Proceedings @LREC2022, pages 16–24
Marseille, 20-25 June 2022

A Comparison of Machine Learning Techniques for Turkish Profanity Detection

Levent Soykan, Cihan Karsak, İlknur Durgar Elkahlout, Burak Aytan
TURKCELL
İstanbul, Turkey
{levent.soykan, cihan.karsak, ilknur.durgar, burak.aytan}@turkcell.com.tr

Abstract

Profanity detection became an important task with the increase of social media usage. Most of the users prefer a clean and profanity free environment to communicate with others. In order to provide a such environment for the users, service providers are using various profanity detection tools. In this paper, we researched on Turkish profanity detection in our search engine. We collected and labeled a dataset from search engine queries as one of the two classes: profane and not-profane. We experimented with several classical machine learning and deep learning methods and compared methods in means of speed and accuracy. We performed our best scores with transformer based Electra model with 0.93 F1 Score. We also compared our models with the state-of-the-art Turkish profanity detection tool and observed that we outperform it from all aspects.

Keywords: Profanity Detection, Natural Language Processing, Text Classification

1. Introduction

Profane language generally contains words or phrases that are disrespectful to someone or something. It may include social, sexual, racial insulting contents. The profane language includes vulgar and swear words, obscene expressions, and naughty jokes etc. With the increase of social media use from all age groups, profanity detection is very crucial on social media content and search engines. Most of the service providers and social media platforms are applying detection and masking methods by content moderation to discourage this type of language. The level of profanity detection can be differ from just censoring succ and f words to a sentiment level. Very simply, one can use blacklists consisting of profanity words and search them in the contents. This approach unfortunately does not satisfy the needs as in most of the cases users can find a way to fool these lists buy making on purpose typos, changing the letter by numbers, using different font types or even emojis. Moreover, there are many words that have dual senses than can both express offense and non-offense meaning depending on the context. An alternative way of profanity detection is employing data-driven methods with classical machine learning and deep learning methods. The task is getting harder when someone works with morphologically complex languages like Turkish.

Recently, automatic profanity detection became one of the trending topics in natural language processing. First attempts was focused on hate speech detection (Chen et al., 2012; Davidson et al., 2017; Agarwal and Sureka, 2017). There are several datasets (Kumar et al., 2018; Ibrohim and Budi, 2018) collected for this purpose and even several shared tasks (Zampieri et al., 2020; Zampieri et al., 2019; Basile et al., 2019) are organized for offensive language and hate speech detection.

In this paper, we focus on Turkish profanity detection on search engine queries. Despite the increasing interest on this topic for other languages, there is still very limited research on Turkish. For our best knowledge there is only one available corpus on Turkish offensive language (Çöltekin, 2020) (approximately 40K Twitter entries). (Çelik and Yıldırım, 2020) is conducted a comparison of classical machine learning techniques for Turkish profanity detection. A dataset (approximately 80K) is also collected within this work but the data is not publicly available yet and the only publicly available profanity tool for Turkish for our best knowledge is Sinkaf [1].

The profanity detection task for Turkish search engine queries is challenging in two respects: the first one is the agglutinative structure of Turkish which brings special difficulties such as sparsity problem. The second is the length of the entities because of the nature of search engine queries. The phrases are very short (three words on average) and classifiers should work with a very limited context.

The first aim of this work is to collect large set of data from search engine queries. We collected a corpus of $400K$ entries [2] and labeled them in one of the two profanity classes (True or False mainly). Then we compared the classification performance of several classical machine learning and deep learning techniques on this dataset. This paper is organized as follows: Section 2 introduces the data collection and labeling processes. In Section 3, we explain the data preprocessing steps. Section 4 and 5 focuses classical machine learning and deep learning model setups and their experimental results. Finally we conclude with Section 6.

[1] https://github.com/eonurk/sinkaf

[2] %50 of the data is freely available for academic purposes. Please contact the authors for dataset acquisition.

2. Data Collection

For data-driven profanity detection to perform well on real world scenarios, it is of crucial importance to have training data that has a similar distribution with the real world data. In order to satisfy this constraint, we carried out an extensive data collection and labeling process and collected a dataset of approximately $400K$ phrases/sentences from search engine queries.

2.1. Labeling Process

We organized a team of twenty people for data labeling. We shared a labeling guide in which we itemized the tagging criteria and provided positive and negative examples. We grouped offense classes into four as *discrimination*, *sexual abuse*, *profanity* and *violence*. Definition of each class is as follows:

- **Discrimination:** All kind of hate speech that includes unjust or prejudicial treatment of different categories of people, especially on the grounds of race, age, sex, or disability.
- **Sexual Abuse:** All kind of phrases that implies any adulty content including unwanted sexual activity like pedophilia.
- Violence: Phrases involving physical force intended to hurt, damage, or kill someone or something.
- **Succ and f words:** Rude and insulting words or phrases to cause someone to feel hurt, angry, or upset including swear words.

We asked annotators to complete a demo task (100 phrases for each annotator) before initializing the main project. By the help of these demo outputs, we revised the labeling guide and finalized the rule set. During the whole process, we employed an in-house labeling and verification tool. Figure 1 shows an example annotation screen used in the study. In the light of the given instructions, the annotator labeled the word *moruk* (geezer) in the phrase *yaşlı moruk* (old geezer) as profanity word and selected the type as **violence**. At the end of the labeling process, all phrases that are labeled in one of the four classes are recorded as True (Profane class) and the rest is recorded as False(not-Profane).

In the first phase of the annotation process was dedicated to the labeling of the entries and in the second phase was used to check the mismatches between annotators and consolidate the output. Randomly selected 10% percent of the data (equally from each annotator) is considered in the consolidation step in which four experts (different from the annotators) checked the wrong labels and words. If all of the labels are correct, it is selected as the final label. If any of the labels or words is wrong, the true label is determined by the expert. Figure 2 illustrates the consolidation screen used in order to analyze the annotations.

(a) Selecting the Profane Phrase

(b) Final View After Labeling

Figure 1: Labeling Example

Figure 2: Annotation Verification

2.2. Corpus Statistics

The total dataset we obtained after labeling process consists of **392,806** phrases. In our dataset, each text input is labeled as False (83.6% of the corpus) and True (16.4% of the coprus). Same distribution is maintained during creation of train/test/validation datasets using Stratified Splits & StratifiedKFold. The longest query has 110 words whereas the shortest one is a single word. Looking at the median values, we can state that the most inputs contain three word sequences and average word length is around six characters. Table 1 illustrates the distribution of query lengths. When tokenized by spaces, whole dataset has over $190K$ unique words, including digits, letters, symbols. This means high dimensionality is an important challenge for this study. The data set created in this study will be made partially publicly available with a permissive license.

In this work, we set aside 10% of entire data as test set and performed data analysis and model training on the 90% of the dataset. For the cases that we need a seperate validation set, 10% of train set is used. Validation is mostly used for model performance evaluation and hyperparameter tuning.

3. Data Preprocessing

In order to clean data, we applied several preprocessing step as shown in Figure 3.

We can briefly explain these preprocessing steps as follows:

- **Lowercasing:** We applied lower casing to all texts in the dataset.

	mean	std	min	25%	50%	75%	max
avg. word length	6.02	2.78	0.31	4.8	5.66	7.0	199
word count	3.09	1.66	1.0	2.0	3.0	4.0	110

Table 1: Corpus Statistics

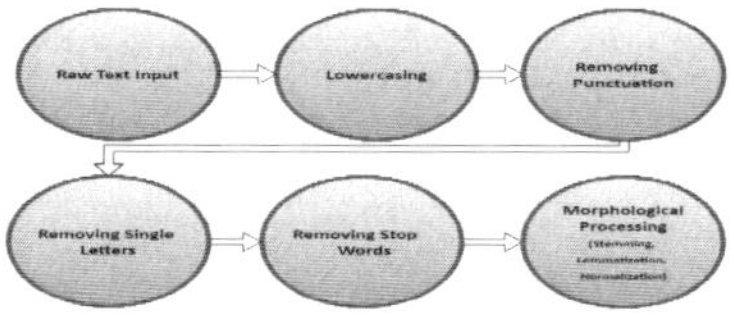

Figure 3: Preprocessing steps applied to the Dataset

- **Punctuation Removal:** As punctuation has a limited effect on profanity, we removed all punctuations.
- **Single Letter Removal:** Although the dataset includes words from different languages, the dominating language is Turkish. Turkish language does not have single letters as words except *o* (he/she/it) which is already in our stop words list. We removed single letters but as digits & numbers may sometimes indicate offense, we kept numeric values untouched.
- **Stop Words Removal:** We removed the stop words using a pre-defined Turkish Stop Words list. These include written numbers, pronouns (demonstratives such as *bu* (this), *şunlar* (these); possessives such as *onun* (his), *benim* (my, mine), reflexive: *kendim* (myself), *kendin* (yourself)) and helping verbs (*yapmak* (to do), *etmek* (to make), etc.). Note that our decision of removing stop words is based on profanity classification. Removal of stopwords may harm other tasks on Turkish such as summarization & sentiment prediction.
- **Morphological Preprocessing/Spellchecking:** We experimented with three morphological processes **i) Normalization:** Basic spell checker and word suggestion. Noisy text normalization applied with Zemberek(Akin, 2019)), **ii)Stemming:** Only Stemming applied after initial preprocessing Tool with TurkishStemmer (Osman Tunçelli, 2019), **iii)Lemmatization:** Only Lemmatization applied after initial preprocessing Tool with Zeyrek[3]. Each process might change the word completely and may also have adverse results.

3.1. Vector Representation of Text Input

Since machine learning tools accept numeric input, a numeric representation of text is required.

processed	normalized	stemmed	lemmatized
181,734	129,532	149,898	151,364

Table 2: Number of word tokens after preprocessing step (Originally: 181,933 tokens)

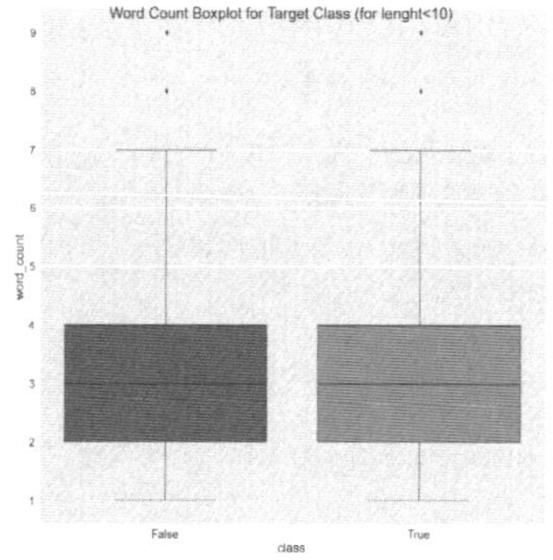

Figure 4: Word Count of the Dataset

Vectorization is a common way of creating numeric features from text data. The most straightforward application is One-Hot-Encoding where all words will be represented as numbers. We used *CountVectorizer* (within scikit-learn) for this step, as it takes care of tokenization and provides n-gram options. Another method is Term Frequency-Inverse Document Frequency (tf-idf), which is based on assigning weights to each token inversely proportional to its frequency across all documents. Tf-idf tokenization helps reduce the effect of stop words/less important words and giving more emphasis to words that are rare and important. By default, vectorization is made using each unique word as a token. However, when grouped together, words might have different meaning or stronger effect. N-Gram Range is a method for grouping all n-word combinations as a single unique token. We represent the comparison of two methods in Section 4.2.

3.2. Feature Selection & Evaluation Metrics

After tokenization and vectorization, our train data has between 120-150K features, and hyperparameter tuning of some ML algorithms with this feature set is inefficient. (especially for tree-based classifiers and ensemble models) For application

[3]https://zeyrek.readthedocs.io/en/latest/

of these models, most relevant features must be identified and data should be represented with fewer features while maintaining the accuracy. To evaluate the dependency of all features and the target variable, we applied Chi2 test, which is a statistical test with the null hypothesis being "the feature and target variable are independent". Test returns a test-statistic and a p-value. For low p-values, we can state that we have enough data to reject the null hypothesis, meaning that the feature is correlated to targets. For our processed data, we have 18.702 unique features that have significant correlation ($p<0.05$) to target. For ensemble models such as RandomForest, this feature set is used.

Since the work might be deployed in profanity detection of online services, a low False Negative rate will be desirable. For this reason, we will use F1 scores mainly as it incorporates both the True-Positive, False-Positive predictions Alongside F1 Score, we will also keep an eye on the recall and precision. Most ML / DL algorithms provide predicted probabilities, where one can also tweak the probability threshold to adjust precision/recall levels. Accuracy could be misleading in imbalanced datasets, but to visualize how a model/pipeline is performing, we can plot a ROC curve. Figure 5 shows a ROC Curve using Logistic Regression. Area under the curve is the main indicator and the diagonal dotted line represents the performance of random guessing where the model cannot distinguish between classes, and as shown in figure, Logistic Regression Model is way above this line.

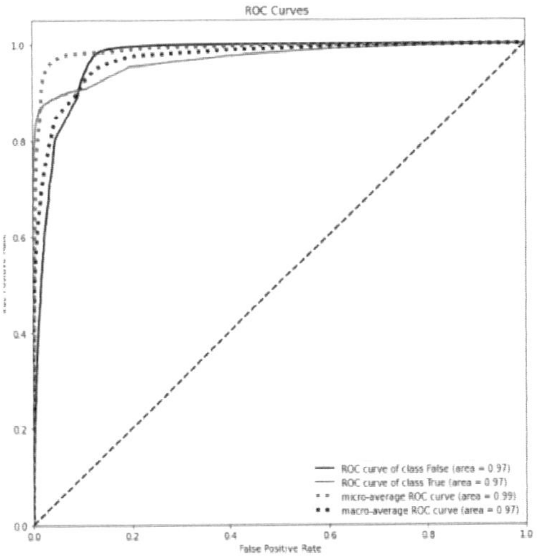

Figure 5: ROC curves for Logistic Regression

4. Classical Machine Learning Experiments

After initial preprocessing, we applied several Machine Learning models to our data.

- **LogisticRegression:** Linear classifier using logistic function (sigmoid curve) to calculate class probabilities. Offers L1-L2 regularization options.
- **SGDClassifier:** A linear classifier applied with Stochastic Gradient Descent where loss is calculated with each sample, and learning rate can be adjusted gradually.
- **LinearSVC:** This model is a faster application of Support Vector Classification with a linear kernel and accepts sparse inputs. The fitting time is much lower compared to standard SVC and is commonly used for text classification.
- **MultinomialNB:** Calculates conditional probability of features, with 'naive' assumption of conditional independence among features.
- **KNeighborsClassifier:** Algorithm based on pre-determined number (k) of nearest data points to each query point.
- **RandomForestClassifier:** Ensemble method fitting a number of Decision Tree Classifiers on sub sample of dataset and averages the outcomes to make predictions. Sub sample size and selection can be controlled with model hyperparameters
- **XGBClassifier:** Uses Gradient Boosting method to combine outputs of a set of Decision Trees where trees are fitted sequentially, and gradient descent is applied for optimization.

4.1. Effect of Morphological Processes

To test the results, we ran the processed data through four ML classification algorithms with default parameters. Table 3 includes the F1-score on 5-fold cross validation of training set with different morphological processes. *Processed* column shows the results with the first four preprocessing steps without morphological preprocessing.

As shown in table 3, it seems that although normalization corrects some spelling errors, it negatively affects total performance, as many misspelled profane words in our dataset are incorrectly changed. The first four preprocessing steps yields good results, lemmatization/stemming can also be tried as they have similar performance. Additional features extracted from text

	processed	normalized	stemmed	lemmatized
SGDClassifier	0.80	0.79	0.82	0.82
LogisticRegression	0.86	0.85	0.87	0.87
LinearSVC	0.91	0.88	0.91	0.91
MultinomialNB	0.81	0.80	0.81	0.81

Table 3: The experimental results with different morphological processes

statistics are not applied, as we did not observe a correlation between these statistics and the target variable. Table 2 shows the final number of unique tokens after preprocessing steps. Figure 4 shows the distribution of word counts.

4.2. Effect of Vectorization

In order to see the effect of vectorization on performance, we performed a cross-validation on LinearSVC model using both Tf-idf & Countvectorizer with Unigram (1,1) and Bi-gram (1,2) options. Table 4 shows the cross validation results. Although the results are close to each other, and CountVectorizer with Unigram seems to work well both in terms of recall and F1-score. Increasing n-gram range does not contribute much, which is somewhat expected as often times profane word can be indicated by a single word. As the performances of ngram-ranges are close, we preferred Counvectorizer with ngram-range(1,1) in the following experiments.

	Cnt(1)	Cnt(2)	Tfidf(1)	Tfidf(2)
Fit T.	7.06	13.25	2.09	3.27
Acc.	0.97	0.97	0.97	0.96
F1	0.91	0.90	0.91	0.89
Recall	0.86	0.84	0.84	0.80

Table 4: Comparison of CountVectorizer and TfidfVectorizer with uni- and bi-grams (fit time in secs)

4.3. ML Experimental Results

Table 5 are the initial results of all models.

As a further step, we applied hyperparameter tuning to LogisticRegression, SGDClassifier, LinearSVC and RandomForestClassifier as shown in Table 6. Best score is achieved by the tuned version of LinearSVC. Classification report and confusion matrix on test set with this model is shown in Table 7. Though there are many False-Positive (Type 1 Error) classifications, the model identifies True (Profane) classes accurately.

5. Deep Learning Methods

After the ML algorithms, we also experimented with deep learning algorithms. We first started with a baseline LSTM model then moved to transformer models BERT and Electra. Finally we tried T5 models.

5.1. Baseline LSTM Model

As a baseline model, we created a two layer LSTM model. We used Keras (Chollet and others, 2015) preprocessing package[4] for preprocessing and Adam (Kingma and Ba, 2015) optimizer, which uses moments calculated with exponentially weighted averages of gradients for optimization. For the loss calculation, we prefered Binary Cross Entropy[5] that uses function uses cross entropy - negative logarithm of predicted probabilities. Our baseline network is created with layers explained in Table 8. The model parameters are as follows:

- Optimizer: AdamW (Learning Rate: 5e-4, weight_decay=1e-3, epsilon: 1e-8)
- GPU Batch Size: 128
- Gradient Clipping: (Max Norm = 2.0)
- Warmup – Linear Schedule with 20.000 steps

5.2. Transformer Models

Transfer Learning is a methodology used in machine learning where the model stores the gained knowledge (updated weights) while training for an objective, and the stored weights are then re-applied with another model to a different problem. This approach is very common in deep learning, where pre-trained models are used and fine-tuned to solve new computer vision and natural language processing problems. The pre-trained models we applied use Transformers(Cho et al., 2014) and Self-Attention(Vaswani et al., 2017) to identify the important parts of text data and learn connections. We use two pre-trained models for our task; BERT(Devlin et al., 2018) & ELECTRA(Clark et al., 2020).

5.2.1. BERT

The main differentiating point of BERT is that it is a Bi-Directional Model. Compared to uni-directional models where context of a word is represented by words to its left (or right), BERT[6] uses context from both sides to represent the words. This is achieved by Masked Language Modelling (MLM)(Song et al., 2019), where

[4]https://www.tensorflow.org/api_docs/python/tf/keras

[5]https://pytorch.org/docs/stable/generated/torch.nn.BCELoss.html

[6]https://github.com/google-research/bert

model	F1	Precision	Recall	Acc.
LogisticRegression	0.87	0.98	0.78	0.96
SGDClassifier	0.80	0.98	0.68	0.95
KNeighborsClassifier	0.74	0.99	0.60	0.93
LinearSVC	0.92	0.98	0.87	0.98
MultinomialNB	0.84	0.88	0.80	0.95
RandomForestClassifier	0.90	0.98	0.85	0.97
XGBClassifier	0.76	0.99	0.61	0.94

Table 5: ML Algoritms Experimental Results

model	F1	Precision	Recall	Acc.
LogisticRegression	0.89	0.98	0.81	0.97
SGDClassifier	0.82	0.91	0.75	0.95
LinearSVC	0.92	0.98	0.87	0.98
RandomForestClassifier	0.91	0.98	0.85	0.97

Table 6: The Effect of Hyperparameter Tuning

Actual vs. Predict	True	False
True	5638	125
False	810	32708

Table 7: Confusion Matrix of LinearSVC the Actual Labels vs Predicted Labels

some words are masked in the input and Transformers are used to predict these masked words. As a pre-trained model, Bert has its own vocabulary and word vectors. The vocabulary is fixed, but BERT has a special word piece tokenization[7]. If the word as a whole does not exist in the vocabulary, the Bert tokenizer splits it into several sub-word segments and trains them separately. This method looks really promising for NLP tasks in Turkish, where there are many possible conjugations of each word, due to the agglutinative nature of the language. Application We used *loodos/bert-base-turkish-uncased*[8] model which has 12 encoder layers with over $30K$ tokens and 768 features on every vector.

- Model Class: BertForSequenceClassification
- Optimizer: AdamW (Learning Rate: 1e-5, epsilon: 1e-8)
- GPU Batch Size: 32
- Gradient Clipping: (Max Norm = 1.0)

5.2.2. Electra

Similar to BERT, Electra also uses Transformer mechanisms, but the main difference is about the training part. Instead of MLM, Electra uses Replaced Token Detection as a task for pre-training. In this task, Electra models[9] are trained to distinguish "real" input tokens vs "fake" input tokens generated by another neural network. After pre-training, the generator network is dismissed and model fine-tuning for new tasks are done only with the discriminator. In experimets, We used *dbmdz/electra-base-turkish-cased-discriminator*[10] which is trained on 35GB corpora including Oscar (Abadji et al., 2022) and Opus corporas(Aulamo et al., 2020). We used the model with the following parameters:

- Model Class: ElectraForSequenceClassification
- Optimizer: AdamW (Learning Rate: 1e-5, weight_decay=1e-2, epsilon: 1e-8)
- GPU Batch Size: 32
- Gradient Clipping: (Max Norm = 1.0)
- Loss Function: BinaryCrossEntropy
- Warmup: Linear Schedule with 20.000 steps.

5.3. T5

T5 (Raffel et al., 2019) model is recently used in various NLP tasks including summarization, classification, question answering, etc. Since it is a sequence-to-sequence model, it is available for our task too. During pre-training objective, the model is trained to predict spans of multiple words as well as single word tokens. This helps the model learn sequential relationships and language structure better. The model has

[7]https://huggingface.co/docs/transformers/tokenizer_summary#wordpiece

[8]https://huggingface.co/loodos/bert-base-turkish-uncased

[9]https://github.com/google-research/electra

[10]https://huggingface.co/dbmdz/electra-base-turkish-cased-discriminator

Layer name	Number of Parameters
Embedding(170913, 500)	85M
LSTM(500,64,numlayers=2,batchfirst=True,drpout=0.5)	16K
Linear(infeatures=64,outfeatures=32,bias=true)	256
Linear(infeatures=32,outfeatures=1,bias=true)	256
Sigmoid()	32768
Dropcout(p=0.5, inplace=False)	512

Table 8: Model Summary

a generate method where it generates IDs, which are then transformed to words by the tokenizer. Therefore, in our study, we received the output as text 'True' – 'False' strings and converted them to numeric 0 and 1 afterwards. We used *mt5-small-turkish-question-paraphrasing* [11] model whic is pre-trained on TQP dataset V0.1 (M. Yusuf Sarıgöz, 2021). We used this model with the following parameters:

- Model Class: T5ForConditionalGeneration
- Optimizer: AdaFactor (Learning Rate: 1e-3)
- GPU Batch Size: 32
- Gradient Clipping: (Max Norm = 1.0)
- Warmup: Linear Schedule with 20.000 steps.

5.4. Experimental Results

Table 9 shows the results of fine-tuned models of deep learning methods on our test data. As seen in the table, our baseline method Classifier Network performs similar to LinearSVC but BERT and ELECTRA performs better than all classical machine learning methods explained in Section 4. We also compared the algorithms from the response time aspect, as depending on the use case, one can sacrifice performance for a faster algorithm. Table 10 shows the inference speed[12] of algorithms for 100 samples from our test data. The average text length of this sample is 18 chars.
We also compared our results with the publicly available Sinkaf tool which is implemented with both classical machine learning and deep algorithms. We selected the same algorithms of Sinkaf that we performed best for both categories (LinearSVC and BERT). As seen in the last two columns of the Table 9, our tool outperforms Sinkaf for both cases.

6. Conclusion

In this work, we focused on Turkish profanity detection of search engine entries. In order to build a model that effectively classifies given text sequences as profane or not-profane, we first collected approximately $400K$ data following a labeling process. Later we applied several classical machine learning algorithms and deep learning models. We compared each approach's performance from both accuracy and speed aspects. Although we have slightly better results with BERT & Electra models (F1 score: 0.93), a default LinearSVC model (F1 score: 0.92) also performs closely to transformer models. This strengthens our first indication after n-gram model comparison that identifying a text as profane/not profane is mostly indicated with single words rather than word groups or contextual meaning/clues. Therefore, simple non-sequential, linear algorithms are almost as effective as deep learning networks for classification of profanity detection. Looking at the predicted validation data, Linear Model missed the True labels if the profane word has an uncommon suffix or joined with another word (by mistake or intentionally). Additional recall performance of Pre-trained Transformer models come from these samples, where sub-word tokenization and embedded vectors helped the model classify these texts more correctly.

[11] https://huggingface.co/dbmdz/electra-base-turkish-cased-discriminator

[12] The configuration of the machine: Intel(R) Core(TM) i7-10750H CPU @ 2.60GHz, 2592 Mhz, 6 Core(s), 12 Logical Processor(s) Installed Physical Memory (RAM), 16,0 GB

7. Bibliographical References

Abadji, J., Ortiz Suarez, P., Romary, L., and Sagot, B. (2022). Towards a Cleaner Document-Oriented Multilingual Crawled Corpus. *arXiv e-prints*, page arXiv:2201.06642, January.

Agarwal, S. and Sureka, A. (2017). Characterizing linguistic attributes for automatic classification of intent based racist/radicalized posts on tumblr micro-blogging website. *CoRR*, abs/1701.04931.

Akin, A. (2019). Zemberek.

Aulamo, M., Sulubacak, U., Virpioja, S., and Tiedemann, J. (2020). OpusTools and parallel corpus diagnostics. In *Proceedings of the 12th Language Resources and Evaluation Conference*, pages 3782–3789, Marseille, France, May. European Language Resources Association.

Basile, V., Bosco, C., Fersini, E., Nozza, D., Patti, V., Rangel Pardo, F. M., Rosso, P., and Sanguinetti, M. (2019). SemEval-2019 task 5: Multilingual detection of hate speech against immigrants and women in Twitter. In *Proceedings of the 13th International Workshop on Semantic Evaluation*, pages 54–63,

model	F1	Precision	Recall	Accuracy
Baseline LSTM	0.92	0.98	0.86	0.97
BERT	0.93	0.96	0.90	0.98
Electra	0.93	0.96	0.89	0.98
T5	0.90	0.94	0.87	0.97
Sinkaf-LinearSVC	0.30	0.75	0.18	0.85
Sinkaf-BERT	0.48	0.80	0.41	0.83

Table 9: Deep Learning Experimental Results

model	mean	std
LinearSVC	171.2ms	8.4ms
Baseline LSTM	231.9ms	17.2ms
BERT	5.0sec	121.8ms
Electra	5.1sec	117.1ms
T5	2.9sec	124.2ms

Table 10: Deep Learning Experimental Results

Minneapolis, Minnesota, USA, June. Association for Computational Linguistics.

Çöltekin, c. (2020). A corpus of turkish offensive language on social media. In *Proceedings of The 12th Language Resources and Evaluation Conference*, pages 6174–6184, Marseille, France.

Chen, Y., Zhou, Y., Zhu, S., and Xu, H. (2012). Detecting offensive language in social media to protect adolescent online safety. In *International Conference on Privacy, Security, Risk and Trust and 2012 International Conference on Social Computing, IEEE*, pages 71–80, 09.

Cho, K., van Merrienboer, B., Gülçehre, Ç., Bougares, F., Schwenk, H., and Bengio, Y. (2014). Learning phrase representations using RNN encoder-decoder for statistical machine translation. *CoRR*, abs/1406.1078.

Chollet, F. et al. (2015). Keras.

Clark, K., Luong, M., Le, Q. V., and Manning, C. D. (2020). ELECTRA: pre-training text encoders as discriminators rather than generators. *CoRR*, abs/2003.10555.

Davidson, T., Warmsley, D., Macy, M., and Weber, I. (2017). Automated hate speech detection and the problem of offensive language. In *Proceedings of ICWSM*, 03.

Devlin, J., Chang, M., Lee, K., and Toutanova, K. (2018). BERT: pre-training of deep bidirectional transformers for language understanding. *CoRR*, abs/1810.04805.

Çelik, A. and Yıldırım, B. (2020). Turkish profanity detection enhanced by artificial intelligence. In *2020 28th Signal Processing and Communications Applications Conference (SIU)*, pages 1–4.

Ibrohim, M. O. and Budi, I. (2018). A dataset and preliminaries study for abusive language detection in indonesian social media. *Procedia Computer Science*, 135:222–229. The 3rd International Conference on Computer Science and Computational Intelligence (ICCSCI 2018) : Empowering Smart Technology in Digital Era for a Better Life.

Kingma, D. P. and Ba, J. (2015). Adam: A method for stochastic optimization. In Yoshua Bengio et al., editors, *3rd International Conference on Learning Representations, ICLR 2015, San Diego, CA, USA, May 7-9, 2015, Conference Track Proceedings*.

Kumar, R., Reganti, A. N., Bhatia, A., and Maheshwari, T. (2018). Aggression-annotated corpus of Hindi-English code-mixed data. In *Proceedings of the Eleventh International Conference on Language Resources and Evaluation (LREC 2018)*, Miyazaki, Japan, May. European Language Resources Association (ELRA).

Osman Tunçelli, Burak Özdemir, H. O. (2019). Turkishstemmer.

Raffel, C., Shazeer, N., Roberts, A., Lee, K., Narang, S., Matena, M., Zhou, Y., Li, W., and Liu, P. J. (2019). Exploring the limits of transfer learning with a unified text-to-text transformer. *CoRR*, abs/1910.10683.

Song, K., Tan, X., Qin, T., Lu, J., and Liu, T. (2019). MASS: masked sequence to sequence pre-training for language generation. *CoRR*, abs/1905.02450.

Vaswani, A., Shazeer, N., Parmar, N., Uszkoreit, J., Jones, L., Gomez, A. N., Kaiser, L., and Polosukhin, I. (2017). Attention is all you need. *CoRR*, abs/1706.03762.

Zampieri, M., Malmasi, S., Nakov, P., Rosenthal, S., Farra, N., and Kumar, R. (2019). Semeval-2019 task 6: Identifying and categorizing offensive language in social media (offenseval). In *Proceedings of the 13th International Workshop on Semantic Evaluation*, pages 75–86.

Zampieri, M., Nakov, P., Rosenthal, S., Atanasova, P., Karadzhov, G., Mubarak, H., Derczynski, L., Pitenis, Z., and Çöltekin, a. (2020). Semeval-2020 task 12: Multilingual offensive language identification in social media (offenseval 2020). In *Proceedings of the 14th International Workshop on Semantic Evaluation*.

8. Language Resource References

M. Yusuf Sarıgöz. (2021). *monatis/tqp: V0.1 (v0.1) Turkish Question Paraphrasing dataset*. Zenodo, ISLRN https://doi.org/10.5281/zenodo.47198011.

Proceedings of the ResT-UP2 Proceedings @LREC2022, pages 25–31
Marseille, 20-25 June 2022

Features and Categories of Hyperbole in Cyberbullying Discourse on Social Media

Simona Ignat*, **Carl Vogel****
**Trinity Centre for Computing and Language Studies
*School of Linguistic, Speech and Communication Scienes
**School of Computer Science and Statistics
{signat, vogel}@tcd.ie

Abstract

Cyberbullying discourse is achieved with multiple linguistic conveyances. Hyperboles witnessed in a corpus of cyberbullying utterances are studied. Linguistic features of hyperbole using the traditional grammatical indications of exaggerations are analyzed. The method relies on data selected from a larger corpus of utterances identified and labelled as "bullying", from Twitter, from October 2020 to March 2022. An outcome is a lexicon of 250 entries. A small number of lexical level features have been isolated, and chi-squared contingency tests applied to evaluating their information value in identifying hyperbole. Words or affixes indicating superlatives or extremes of scales, with positive but not negative valency items, interact with hyperbole classification in this data set. All utterances extracted has been considered exaggerations and the stylistic status of "hyperbole" has been commented within the frame of new meanings in the context of social media.

Keywords: cyberbullying, hyperbole

1. Introduction

Hyperbole has deep roo ts in the poetry of antiquity as a source of emotion. Quintilian defined this poetic device in Institutio Oratoria, as "the elegant straining of the truth, for exaggeration or attenuation" (Book 8, Chapter 6). Use of hyperbole in other contexts has been discussed as a potential threat to truth and objective information for professional groups like journalists (Ireton and Posettie, 2018, p. 56). Broader risks also emerge in the context of defamation, and harassment.
The "rhetorical hyperbole" concept, based on a non-truth, is used in American law system. Although it cannot be used as evidence, the "rhetorical hyperbole" exists as concept, based on the First Amendment to the US Constitution, as conveyance for the "freedom of speech" (Smolla, 2006, p. 715). Hyperbole has become a source of fear, intimidation, threat, bullying for naming just few outcomes on new media. This paper reports reflections on hyperbole as emerges from the linguistic analysis of bullying in online communications.

2. Related work

Natural language hyperbole is evidently frequent, but the phenomenon is not extensively studied (Claridge, 2011; Cano Mora, 2009). A semantic taxonomy has been proposed (Cano Mora, 2009), emphasising the disseminations between positive - negative effects on one side and quantity – quality on the other. An exaggeration in quantity or quality has been outlined (Ferré, 2014, p. 33), identifying two types of verbal- lexical hyperboles, "using a word which is very close or equals the maximal degree on the scale", and a second type based on "changing the predicate to another one (...) which is thus highly unexpected in that context". Claridge (2011) distinguishes between conventional, semi-creative (or semi-conventional) and creative hyperbole. The importance of hyperbole on "presenting objectively reality is a challenge for social media" (Brantly, 2020, p. 90). A procedure for identification of hyperbole based on patterns has been proposed with the HIP method (Burgers et al., 2016) based on eliminating the possibility of being irony or metaphor. The authors identified four characteristics based on literature review of definitions, meaning exaggeration, overstatement, extremity, and/or excess. In 2018, a team of researchers created Hypo, a dataset with "exaggerations" for "automatic hyperbole detection" (Troiano et al., 2018, p.3296). The dataset has been selected on the criteria of "imageability" which is "the degree to which a word can evoke a mental image" and "unexpectedness refers to the fact that hyperboles are less predictable expressions than literal" (Troiano et al., 2018, p.3301). The conclusion was that most "conventional hyperboles" are impossible to detect. The authors use alternatively "exaggerations" and "hyperboles" for nominating the first ones with possible stylistic effect, thus becoming "hyperboles". Compared to other figures of speech like simile, metaphor, metonymy, the hyperbole has been argued to be harder to detect: "hyperbole poses a further difficulty-unlike simile, alliteration or some other figures of speech, it is *unmarked*, that is, it has no linguistic sign to alert the reader to its presence" (Connor, 2019, p. 15). The research reported here is also corpus driven, based on a novel corpus drawn from online communications.

3. Methods

A corpus of 4100 of utterances with bullying effect has been extracted from Twitter following the definitions of bullying used within United States, European Union and Irish legislation, and informed by considerations raised in academic papers.

The linguistic conveyances of bullying have been identified for each utterance. For example, the utterance with bullying effect "this is such a shitty it competes with my shittiest shits" has been identified on the criterion "squalid language". The clause repeats derivatives from the same root "shit", a taboo lexical item and evokes tautology by comparing two superlatives. In the same way, utterances having hyperbole as conveyance for embedding the bullying effect have been identified.

The first question is what utterances could be labelled as hyperboles by using the traditional grammatical indications of exaggerations. This aim has been achieved by labelling utterances with a various range of meanings as exaggerated against a reference considered average, under the criteria of a "reasonable person" nominated by United States legislation. The legislative criterion is used because it can be regarded as a settled convention. The 2013 Code of Alabama Title 13A – Criminal Code, 2010 Nevada Code, and Georgia Code Title 20 use "the reasonable person" thinking as the reference for labelling "hyperbole" in the dataset.[1][2][3]

The exaggerations have been identified by using a behavioural frame convention defined as "a standard that, though it does not demand perfection, does insist upon a certain level of prudence and attentiveness to the interests of others" (Moran, 2003, p. 18). An extended discussion argues about "commonness of hyperbole in everyday spontaneous spoken language" (Claridge, 2011, p. 2) and arises the question about the stylistic effect in cyberbullying discourse. Conversely, what utterances are exaggerations without being necessarily hyperbole, and this is the second question of the document. For answering to it, the whole spectrum of linguistic conveyances has been considered for discovering the triggers of bullying effect by exaggeration. A lexical - semantic analysis has been applied in the first instance and wide topics like "Exaggerations of physical features", "Murder", or "Religion" have been identified.

The 4100 items analysed here are available for others to analyze.[4] Each item is classified by the first author using a fixed range of labels, with each item potentially supporting multiple labels. Lexical items were isolated independently of the classification of items in the dataset as appropriately categorized as hyperbole or not. Spaces were used as indicated (e.g "est ") in order to assure a word initial or word final observation for prefixes and suffixes, where this interacts with interpretation (e.g., "estimate" does not indicate a superlative). The counting method entails that where prefixes are shared ("no", "no one", "noone"), the counts are not independent. We constructed a contingency table that assures independence of row counts (i.e. only " no" counts are used of the three items mentioned in the preceding parenthetical).

Issues in identifying the hyperboles have been found in structures like metaphor, irony, simile, epithet. In disseminating hyperboles over other linguistic conveyances, the predominant feature of exaggeration and both figurative and literal meanings have been considered. The method here is largely observational. The goal is to provide an indication of the linguistic devices that achieve hyperbole particularly in the context of online bullying.

4. Results

The total count of items for each label is as in Table 1, below. We identify a small number of lexical forms, affixes and strings that may also appear as or within words, that indicate superlatives or scalar extremes.

Item	Type	Obs. = 1	Obs. = 2	Compl.
"est "	suffix	43		4057
"most"	word	24		4076
"least"	word	2		4098
"only"	word	18	1	4081
"all"	word	217	13	3870
" any"	prefix	39		4061
"every"	word	67		4033
"never"	word	33	1	4066
" no"	prefix	285	5	3810
"noone"	word	1		4099
"no one"	word	39		4061
" die"	word	56		4044
"death"	word	6		4094

Table 1: Marks of exaggeration: The count of messages with 1 or 2 observations (obs.) of types paired with the count of the complement – tokens in the message that are not the instances of the type at the relevant row.

The chi-squared statistic (df = 11) is 58.84, p = 1.521e-08. Thus, one may accept the hypothesis that there is an interaction between the classification of tokens

[1]2013 Code of Alabama Title 13A - CRIMINAL CODE. Chapter 11 - OFFENSES AGAINST PUBLIC ORDER AND SAFETY. Article 1 - Offenses Against Public Order and Decency." n.d. Justia Law. https://law.justia.com/codes/alabama/2016/title-13a/chapter-11/article-1/section-13a-11-8> – last verified May 2022.

[2]2010 Nevada Code Title 15 CRIMES AND PUNISHMENTS Chapter 200 Crimes Against the Person NRS 200.575. Stalking: Definitions; penalties." n.d. JUSTITIA US Law 2010. https://law.justia.com/codes/nevada/2010/title15/chapter200/nrs200-575.html – last verified May 2022.

[3]Georgia Code Title 20. Education § 20-2-751.4. n.d. FindLaw For Legal Professionals. https://codes.findlaw.com/ga/title-20-education/ga-code-sect-20-2-751-4.html – last verified May 2022.

[4]Please send email to the first author to request a copy.

Item	Hyperbole +	Hyperbole -
"est "	16	225
"most"	8	16
"least"	0	2
"only"	3	17
"all"	16	227
" any"	6	48
"every"	14	53
"never"	4	31
" no"	37	468
"noone"	0	1
"no one"	2	37
" die"	4	61
"death"	1	5
Complement	1523	19903

Table 2: Marks of exaggeration: The count of relevant items (or all other items as the "Complement" in the final row") in messages marked as containing hyperbole compared with the counts of the same lexical types in messages not marked as containing hyperbole.

in the dataset as containing hyperbole and the counts of items indicated in Table 2. To note the role of each item, inspection of residuals is revealing (see Table reft:residuals). Recall that the sign of residuals indicates the direction of divergence between observed counts and the counts that would be expected if there were no interaction between the classification of an item as hyperbole and the counts of indicated items (positive values indicate observations in excess of expectations; negative values indicate fewer than expected observations), and the magnitude indicates significance (for magnitudes between 2 and 4, $p < 0.05$; greater than 4, $p < 0.001$).

	Residuals	
Item	Hyperbole +	Hyperbole -
"est "	2.79159150	-0.776979672
"most"	4.776562572	-1.329453833
"least"	-0.379202193	0.105542804
"only"	1.302644859	-0.362563281
"all"	-0.351929761	0.097952107
" any"	1.311433836	-0.365009505
"every"	4.183947046	-1.164512000
"never"	0.935248183	-0.260306290
" no"	0.823021834	-0.229070491
" die"	0.003639818	-0.013077415
"death"	0.865741911	-0.240960709
complement	-0.44319369	0.12335028

Table 3: Residuals

It can be seen that the significant effects are for items that indicate positive extremes ("est", "most", "every", as opposed to "least", "no, "never"). That is, the data revealed a higher number of "maximise" utterances, utterances that emphasize the extreme large end of a scale, than "minimise" utterances that focus on the extreme small end of a scale. However, on a scale of arguments, within the lexical units in the dataset, both labels are variables depending on the perspective of measurement.

4.1. Exaggerations of physical features

The topics of exaggerations cover a complex spectrum of subjects, focused on person or group. Both literal and figurative meanings have been considered, if simultaneously present, for labelling the hyperboles. The next sections provide examples of dimensions of focus in abusive hyperbole witnessed in the corpus. Linguistic features of the constructions are highlighted.

4.1.1. Overweight

The individual is bullied by oversizing the physical body-parts as a compound noun "belly-to-the-ground". Labelling a person "the fat pig" is an allusion to somebody who eats large quantities of food in a non-discretionary way. The ironical allusion "you need wheels on flaps" suggests the requirement of an extra device for carrying own body due to excess weight. The bullying allusions to overweight are based on the presumption of banning the fat people from society.

4.1.2. Ugliness

The causal connection between the aesthetics of physical features and behavioural choices is in most cases tenuous. Thus, stating "if u ignored this ur ugly" is exaggerated and intimidating. Extending the ugliness of an individual over the place of living and indirectly over habitants of the space, as the synecdoche 'ugly ass hometown' implies, is unfair and exaggerated.

4.1.3. Non-visual Senses

Exaggerations based on the sensory perception of an individual frequently attend to smell and taste. It could be the olfactive sense as "you smell like shit", an exaggeration unless the person accidentally fell in that matter. The utterance "you tasteless piece of shit" could be a disgusting perspective if the words have a literal interpretation or a taboo way of offending somebody by outlining the worthiness of person if the figurative meaning is considered.

4.1.4. Mutilations

Data revealed utterances embedding physical mutilations possible in real life but belonging to a wild and long-gone dark Medieval Age if commented on literal meaning, like "have his limbs ripped off", "you were rosted" or "I was fucking the shit out of this guy". These were torture methods. Some of them became metaphors by a figurative interpretation, like "you were roasted" for emphasising a difficult situation for a person. The threat "you're gonna eat your words" embeds an abstract element in a concrete activity.

4.1.5. Overpowering actions

Physical actions, either literally or figuratively interpreted, over a person's body, as in the utterance "fuck yourself. Forever, ideally" are impossible to do continuously. Overpowering actions commanded over the body of victim, like "fuck yourself in the humblest way" is a hyperbole as the adjective "humble" does not have a reference scalar in real life, and it is purely subjective. An overpowering statement "you should tie your tubes now", a suggestion of requiring permanent birth control is an overstatement of what one person may reasonably impose unwillingly on another.

Emphasis on the resources consumed by an target, like "you are a waste of New York air" or "you're no good for the planet" has a double possible interpretation as physical and psychological destruction can be used to in an exaggerated form to achieve bullying.

4.1.6. Stalking

Intimidation based on permanent stalking, action impossible to be done in real life, unless a physical symbiosis is accomplished, is exemplified by utterances like "I'll always be listening for your voice", "I'll never leave your side", or "no matter how far you run I'll find you".

4.1.7. Murder

A whole spectrum of various imaginary forms of killing somebody has been revealed by the data. The suicidal imperatives like "go kill urself" or "dump chemicals into the mouth" posted on social media suggest an infringement of each individual right over own life. The utterance "pull out your intestines" is an indirect urge to suicide in an aggressive way. The utterance "everyone should die" does not even specify the reason of mass extinction and includes the author too in human race's destruction, thus this is an indirect wish of suicide.

Urges to mass extinctions of a nation like the imperatives "kill jews", "kill faggots" are impossible to be achieved by a single person. Hyperboles embedding the message of mass extinction are achieved by anchoring extremes in abstract triggers like categories of humans or attitudes towards humans (e.g., respect). An example of the former is "*Race* stinks therefore should die", and of the later, "try to disrespect my son I will beat the living out of you". Bullying exaggerations based on nationalities put an unfair stigma over all people having the citizenship of a country. Sometimes, murderous imperatives are suggested with no explicit reason at all like "kill all men".

An utterance embedding medical jargon, "these vaccines are killing millions", is not based on scientific evidence as people could die from many other reasons. Reasons of selecting the people who should die are sometimes humorous: "people with nice noses should die".

4.2. Exaggerations of moral features

Bullying exaggerations can be achieved via comparison of person against hypothetical worst persons in the world and labelled her or him as a "winner" of such a competition. Examples are: "you are the worst candidate in history", "your one of the worst human beings I've ever heard", "you are one of the worst human beings on earth". The adjective "horrid" in the sentence "ur the most horrid person" has similar effect, involving adjectival modification rather than a nominal. These comparisons are impossible to achieve in a literal and truthful sense, given the subjectivity of the underlying categorization.

Self-esteem is targeted by sentences starting by personal pronoun "you", embedding an imperative message, focused on superlative structures, with two subcategories. The first subcategory implies a comparison and encompasses utterances like "you are a despicable human being", "you're childish asf", "you're a sociopath and a disgrace to the human race", "you are one of the the biggest fool", "you're a sociopath and a disgrace to the human race", "you are one of the worst human beings on this planet", or "you are one of the worst human beings walking the earth". The aggressor declares a superlative level which cannot be proved in a literal sense because there is no accepted scale of measurement. The second category implies a reference to an abstraction or no reference at all. For the first subcategory of these, an example is "everything you say is slutty or dumb" and for the second, an example is "you should think of yourself a failure". The utterances "you never were good" and "you don't deserve anything" are overpowering and suggest a self-comparison in which the target fares poorly. The same idea of superlative is conveyed by utterance "your hypocrisy is gigantic" with abstract - noun references qualified by an adjective of quantity.

The utterance "all you think about is yourself" implies that the target is an egocentric person. These posts about victim's interactions with other people is bullying as they are based upon speculation, for example "u feel like everyone hates you" or "your desperate for views". Within this set, the utterances "everyone": "every1 abandons you", "every1 who hates u is weird", "everyone hates you", "everyone step on you", reveal a double presupposition, the first on other people's thoughts and the second about victim's feelings. These utterances covering speculative actions, thoughts or emotions of a person, posted on social media, could have a bullying effect. An exaggeration of person's actions by using a metaphor, "look like your typical backstabbing" to describe a deviously vengeful personality.

4.3. Religion

Religion is invoked through reference to deities. For example, "X was a satanic psychopathic" broadly describes a bad character with mental disorder without specific features but labelled as a human being requiring medical attention. The exclusion of individual on the criterion of sin in a dramatic way is hyperbolic, as in utterance "the worse sinners is shamed of u". This utterance outlines ironically the failure of reaching the lowest level of sin which is an abstract notion already banned. Sin itself is an abstract notion, variable to religion, thus the label "the worse sinners" is undetermined in any literal sense.

Presupposing the existence of "approved altars" in the utterance "you don't worship at approved altars" implies a restriction of the fundamental right of choice in beliefs assumed in contemporary society.

The utterance "you're a wretched sinner" implies the impossible redemption, but the reference, the sin, itself has no objective framework and therefore redemption does not have a literal reference either.

An aggressor's claim to extraordinary powers over life and death is conveyed by sentences "those who are truthful will survive my wrath". This statement evokes apocalyptic prophecy.

The derogatory imperative against a deity from the utterance "fuck your God" is exaggerated against the respectful attitude civil society expects to be shown to each person's spiritual values.

All these exaggerations meant to intimidate and to emotionally damage the individual targeted.

4.4. Exaggerations based on gender

Derogatory gender-oriented labels are evident in the data with application either to women, as "she's plain and simply a homophobic horror" and to men labelled as "useless". In social media, people are labelled in a derogatory way based on gender orientation as in "queer person is an abomination" or "straights are awful". Criticising a person for having something as naturally occurring in human beings as gender appears to be exaggeration.

4.4.1. Statements against men

Data revealed two categories of hyperboles against men if the criterion of referentiality is applied. These are statements with indeterminate referent and clear reference respectively. Statements with indeterminate referent are sometimes offered as generics, addressing the whole group of individuals designated as "male" in exaggeration because not all individuals have the same characteristics. For example, "big dick men know when to shut the fuck up" has the form of a natural language generic but invokes two exaggerated categories. Examples like "trash men are exactly why sexual abuse is a problem", or "the shitty men are always offended" include a term ("trash" or "shitty") that lack literal reference. As adjectives, the labels applied to people are hyperbolic as they do not have a scale of reference. Pointing against one gender or other and making accusations without proof is an exaggeration (e.g. "men are the root of all problems").

The utterance "men are useless" is an exaggeration because "utility" is an abstraction defined subjectively according to own needs and not all men are completely "useless." A subjective reference is involved in the statement "men are so worthless" as "worthy" is a subjective scale of appreciating a person. The exaggeration becomes a hyperbole if posted on social media as it appears intended to offend all men who read the message. These claims about all men on planet are sometimes evidently intended to extend the impact of a judgement of a specific individual. A statement like "boys are mostly assholes" could be interpreted as most of boys are assholes or each boy is mostly asshole and less non-asshole. Neither statements can be objectively proven, thus they are speculations aiming to intimidate. Stating equivalence between two distinct referents is frequently hyperbolic. For example, "somebody wants world peace it's freaking gay" or "this school doesnt give schlrshps its freakin gay". This series continue in the same manner with utterances "steamed hams it's freaking gay", "contact lenses. It's freaking gay on you", "ending every sentence with an smiley face. It's Freaking gay". An irrelevant and exaggerated connection between random elements or activities and gay people is bullying.

4.4.2. Statements against women

A group of texts mentioned a "woman's card" required for validating something already assigned from birth, for example "women (...) have revoked your woman's card", "you need to have your woman card cut up". The rhetorical question "how much of a slut" conveys the superlative focussing on degrees of membership in the named nominal category, but with an implicit suggestion that "partial" membership in the derogatory category results in "total" membership. Similarly, in "she is a completely massive irredeemable cunt", the taboo "cunt" is a metonymy without natural graduations. Labelling a person "bitch" because she "calls and leaves no message" is unfair and unrealistic as there are many people who calls and leave no messages because different reasons.

In conclusion, gender seems to be a controversial locus of hyperbole since the authors on social media post statements accusing the different genders, ultimately, of being themselves. They criticised all men and women, briefly, "straights are awful", or all people labelled on criterion of sexual orientation, "you are biphobic" as a total rejection of everybody.

4.5. Statement with indeterminate reference

4.5.1. Exaggerated consequences of actions

The intimidating effect is triggered by exaggerations of consequences like "if you say anything else on the topic I murder you" or "murder you bc of that emoji". A metaphoric utterance, "your voice bring disease" is an exaggeration in terms of literal interpretation, but a truth based on facts if the virus is spread via speaking. Threatening a person with physical harm for minor reasons is an overreaction, like "i beat the living shit out of this girl for not giving me my food frm door dash", "I will beat the living shit out of who breaks the rules" or "I will beat someone who touches my food". An unjustified death punishment suggested by utterance "people who don't like indian food should die". Gastronomical preferences generally should not be a criterion for punishment, much less death. Food is the topic of an exaggerated threat in this clause: "if someone spiking someone else's drink beat the living shit out of them". Exaggerations based on relative age – behaviour with a difference between what is it expected and what person shows "am Scottish alot maturer than you are!", "How immature for not minding your own business". There are no widely known statistics about Scottish people being more or less mature than other people, and minding somebody else business is a widely practice among all age – groups. Thus, it is unfair to connect a late childhood to the exaggerated interest shown by a victim towards other people's activities. An unfair sign of immaturity is labelled also the discussion about somebody's mother in utterance "how immature to talk about somebody's mom". People often talk about members of other families, this is not necessarily a sign of immaturity. An exaggeration is also the accusation of making the social media toxic as in exclamation "You're the reason social media is so toxic". Social media is made of opinions coming from various people. Claiming that one person is responsible for the totality of online offensiveness is a false exaggeration.

4.5.2. Exaggerations by a group

The bully states a presupposition about the thoughts of a group as in "no one wants you" or "no one in America wants to hear from you". These statements, based on overpowering attitude on behalf of all group without having precise information about the opinion of each member, are exaggerations with bullying effect. The presupposition about an action made by a group of deceased people, like "our founders would puke at our cowardliness" is derogatory and exaggerated. Within the same area of tagging unfairly a state or symbols of it are "US existence is a crime" and "US flag is a nazi flag". Bullying is also labelling somebody for the group to which belong the person, a sin utterance "your democratic assholes". Telling somebody about a mass rejection is false and intimidating but not true. This message is conveyed in the dataset by indefinite pronoun "every1" spelled as an internet slang word or regular spelling in utterances "every1 abandons you", "everyone hates you" or "everyone step on you". The same group – rejection is also suggested by negative pronoun in the utterance "no one wants you". An exaggeration stating the ownership of a state conveyed by the metonymic "my state" from utterance "don't come to my state", cannot be true administratively in a republic form of government. On social media, the concept of "group" could have the meaning of followers of a person. A possible blackmail method is used by stating an information as known by whole group, but being a false, for example "the entire timeline knows". Inducing the fear of making public a personal information from victim's life without applying this threat in real world is an intimidating exaggeration.

5. Discussion and Conclusions

The speech act of exaggeration within the bullying has aggressor and victim "assuming" necessarily a specific role. If X is aggressor and Y is victim, then exaggeration happens if Y takes the message as such, whereas the intention of X was. Therefore, exaggeration relies exclusively on a subjective perception of bullied – victim.

Hyperbole is a figure of speech with deep roots into poetical emotion. The question is whether any lyricism has been left into hyperbole used on social media. The dataset for hyperbole has been selected from bullying discourse utterances from social media, thus the chances to connect lyricism to bullying are very small. Hyperbole in social media is connected to satiric poetry reaching sometimes the invective to an extreme squalid language.

Hyperboles, as exaggerations, typically imply scales, and maximum or minimum points on such scales. Examples have been provided of maximising and minimising utterances although the last ones could cross the understatement, another figure of speech. However, the understatement is an "undersize" in the way of presentation, but not in the meaning transmitted by message. Therefore, all undersize and oversize meanings have been considered exaggerations or hyperboles.

Exaggeration is a source of bullying on social media. Making the individual to feel weak, big, excessive in consumption, ugly, mentally disordered and in any other way unwanted and very close to wishing one's own death, by posting such false statements on social media is bullying.

Hyperbole conveys a "strong emotion from reader" whereas "reader" is an aggressor or a victim. This is a topic open for discussions on the criteria of multiple variables crossing centuries and human perception. This document is aiming to enrich the data on hyperboles on new media in an attempt to an automatic foreseen detection of harmful content.

6. Bibliographical References

Brantly, A. (2020). Beyond hyperbole: The evolving subdiscipline of cyber conflict studies. *The Cyber Defense Review*, 5(3):99–119.

Burgers, C., Brugman, B. C., de Lavale tte, K. Y. R., and Steen, G. J. (2016). Hip: A method for linguistic hyperbole identification in discourse. *Metaphor and Symbol*, 31(3):163–178.

Cano Mora, L. (2009). All or nothing: A semantic analysis of hyperbole. *Revista de Lingüística y Lenguas Aplicadas*, 4(1).

Claridge, C. (2011). *Hyperbole in English: A Corpus-based Study of Exaggeration*. Cambridge, UK: Cambridge University Press.

Connor, W. R. (2019). When hyperbole enters politics: What can be learned from antiquity and our hyperbolist-in-chief. *Arion: A Journal of the Humanities and the Classics*, 26(3):15–32.

Ferré, G. (2014). Multimodal hyperbole. *Multimodal Communication*, 3(1):25–50.

Ireton, C. and Posettie, J. (2018). Journalism 'fake news' & disinformation: Handbook for journalism education and training. Pris: United Nations Educational, Scientific and Cultural Organization.

Moran, M. (2003). *Rethinking the Reasonable Person: An Egalitarian Reconstruction of the Objective Standard*. Oxford: Oxford University Press.

Smolla, R. A. (2006). Group libel. In Paul Finkelman, editor, *Encyclopedia of American Civil Liberties*, page 715. New York: Routledge.

Troiano, E., Strapparava, C., Özbal, G. S., and Tekirogl, S. (2018). A computational exploration of exaggeration. In *Proceedings of the 2018 Conference on Empirical Methods in Natural Language Processing*, pages 3296–3304.

Author Index